POST-AUTISM

POST-AUTISM

A Psychoanalytical Narrative

with supervisions by Donald Meltzer

by

Marisa Pelella Mélega

published for
The Harris Meltzer Trust
by
KARNAC

Published in 2014 for The Harris Meltzer Trust
by Karnac Books Ltd, 118 Finchley Road, London NW3 5HT

Some chapters published in Portuguese in 1999 by Imago, Rio de Janeiro, as *Pós-Autismo: Uma Narrativa Psicanalítica*

Translated by Henrik Carbonnier
English editing by Nalini Jain and Meg Harris Williams

British Library Cataloguing in Publication Data
A C.I.P. for this book is available from the British Library

ISBN 978 1 78049 139 4

Edited, designed and produced by The Bourne Studios
www.bournestudios.co.uk
Printed in Great Britain

www.harris-meltzer-trust.org.uk
www.karnacbooks.com

CONTENTS

About the authors   vii

Foreword   ix

1   *Mário and his stories*   1

2   *Applying the post-Kleinian understanding of autistic states*   21

3   *Technical problems of the analysis*   43

4   *Fighting the use of autistic objects*   71

5   *Mário reaches adolescence*   89

6   *Review*   103

References   115

Index   117

Marisa Pelella Mélega is a psychiatrist, psychoanalyst in private practice, and a Training Analyst and Supervisor at the Brazilian Psychoanalytic Society of São Paulo. She founded the São Paulo Mother–Baby Relationship Study Centre in 1987, receiving accreditation from the Centro Studi Martha Harris, in Rome. She teaches at the Brazilian Institute as a child psychoanalyst, where she chaired the training in child analysis from 1990 to 1996. Her clinical and research interests include applications of the Esther Bick observation model, as in assessment and therapeutic interventions with parents and children. She is the author of *Eugenio Montale, Poetic Creativity and Psychoanalysis* (L'Atelier, 2001), and co-editor of *Looking and Listening: Work from the São Paulo Mother–Baby Relationship Study Centre* (Harris Meltzer Trust, 2012).

Email: pmelega@uol.com.br

Donald Meltzer (1923–2004) practised as a psychiatrist in the United States before moving to England to have analysis with Melanie Klein, becoming a training analyst for the British Society. He worked with both adults and children, and was innovative in the treatment of autistic children; his earlier work with children was supervised by Esther Bick, with whom he started a Kleinian study group after Klein's death. Meltzer taught child psychiatry and psychoanalytic history at the Tavistock Clinic. He is the author of many books, including *The Psychoanalytical Process* (1967), *Sexual States of Mind* (1973), *Explorations in Autism* (1975), *Dream Life* (1983), *The Apprehension of Beauty* (1988; with Meg Harris Williams), and *The Claustrum* (1992). *The Kleinian Development* (1978) and *Studies in Extended Metapsychology* (1986) pioneered the understanding of the theoretical context and clinical relevance of the work of Wilfred Bion. Meltzer taught widely abroad and his books have been published in many languages.

S everal factors have motivated the publication of this narrative of the structuring of a personality in a child who suffered from an untreated condition of infantile autism. The first is a wish to share with the reader interested in psychoanalysis the intimacy of an analytical process in which the quality of the human relationship and the peculiarities of the world where such children live make the task of analysing them extremely hard and, sometimes, impossible. I also wish to share the supervision process performed by Donald Meltzer during a four year period from 1979 to 1983.

In 1975, Donald Meltzer and collaborators published *Explorations in Autism: A Psychoanalytical Study*, which reports the ten years' work experience (1960-1970) of a group of therapists supervised by Meltzer, who analysed children presenting with early infantile autism. The author describes how during the work a new vision of autism emerged that differed greatly from any previously suggested in the psychoanalytical and psychiatric literature. Before 1978 however, the date when I started sessions with Mário, texts about autism were not known in São Paulo.

The treatment of disturbances in the emotional development of children aged three years and under was just beginning - the period in which autistic defences of psychogenetic origin first become noticeable.

In the first year of analysis (four times a week), I had all kinds of difficulty in establishing an analytic situation, although Meltzer states in his book that, in essence, the analysis of an autistic child does not differ technically from the analysis of children as described by Melanie Klein, and is based on the systematic investigation of the transference. Mário's behaviour as described by his parents suggested an autistic withdrawal of psychogenetic origin. There was an unsatisfactory mother-infant relationship in which the sensuality and the possessiveness of the child's disposition induced a strong tendency to fusion with the maternal object. This led to a failure of the containing function of the external object (mother) and, consequently, to a failure of the capacity for self-containment.

The history of Mário's psychomotor development does not suggest encephalopathy as a determining factor of his autistic manifestations, but the continuous medication with neuroleptics and antipsychotics from two to twelve years surely had a harmful effect on his development. I would appeal to professionals who deal with the age group from infancy to three years that, on recognising the specific features of this mental condition, they refer children to specialized professionals with a background in mother-infant observation, autism and infantile psychosis, and who are familiar with psychoanalytical methodology.

From the beginning, Mário presented himself as a kind of reporter, a Biblical story teller, talking nonstop from beginning to end of the session, and not willing to be interrupted by my talk, leaving no space for my existence. What kind of relationship could he establish? What was the nature of his transference? were the questions I repeatedly asked myself.

In August 1979, I had my first supervision with Donald Meltzer and Martha Harris at the Brazilian Psychoanalytic Society in São Paulo, and from that time my comprehension of the autistic world into which Meltzer had penetrated deepened, locating the mysterious phenomena of the human mind that operated on these children in a condensed manner. Meltzer writes at the end of the first chapter of *Explorations:* "These phenomena, of dismantling, impairment of special and temporal concepts, employment of mindlessness as a temporising move – all these seem to us to throw a very bright beam on modes of thought and relationship discernible elsewhere, in normal or ill people, in the analytic consulting room as in everyday life" (1975, p. 5). The great impact on this analysis was with my own countertransference feelings to the boy who projected onto me his "moribund baby" state of mind, while he assumed a "gorilla" state (disguised as a reporter-commentator-actor), obstructing all the contact between baby and mother, patient and analyst. In the following narrative may be seen my attempts and manoeuvres to open up a space for communication, and all the strategies for trying to make contact with the baby, since access towards Mário's mind could hardly be made through the "gorilla".

Emotionally the analysis was very costly, owing to the extensive obsessive organization of the autistic state. When Mário was two years old, the time the autistic state became manifest, he received no psychological therapy. When he came to analysis ten years later, a great part of his psychic potential to develop a symbolic mind was lost.

However I believe I received brilliant lessons from Donald Meltzer that have enlarged my general psychoanalytical capacity to investigate the transference and countertransference. With Mário I learned better to observe facts of both behaviour and emotion during the session, to avoid sticking exclusively to verbalizations, and to search for my own oneiric images during the sessions in order to make analysing him possible.

Since that time what has expanded in Brazil and Argentina, as also in other countries, is the vision of parent-child interaction based on Esther Bick's observational method. This vision has enabled the evaluation and diagnosis of autistic signs and modes of behaviour in babies and young children where early intervention has led to a more promising evolution.

Finally, I want to make public my immense admiration for Donald Meltzer's clinical work, his deep understanding of the mind and his great ability to theorize his discoveries. With him I have learned much about the practice of psychoanalysis and to him I dedicate this book.

CHAPTER ONE

Mário and his stories

Mário was referred to me aged eleven years and nine months, and his treatment lasted around seven years, monitored over most of that time by Donald Meltzer, with a review of the case eighteen years later. The following narrative will demonstrate the steps taken toward building an analytical relationship with the boy, and testify to the analyst's emotions in the face of the difficulty of establishing a link that could evolve into a growth relationship. When Mário came to me for analysis, I knew that he had severe difficulties in getting in touch with reality and a strong learning disorder and, when he was almost two years old, presented with autistic behaviour, according to a clinical assessment made by a neurologist at the time.

Mário's developmental history

From the very beginning of his life Mário's fragility in his object relations was clear: he had difficulty in taking his mother's nipple, took too long to suck; his mother had the impression that he didn't like feeding until at two years of age, he started to be fed with a bottle. During the first three months, he cried his eyes out, day and night, apparently due to colic. Then he would calm down and wherever his mother placed him he stayed calm, provided she was close to him. His mother reports that she didn't hold him on her lap except at feeding time, so that he wouldn't get in the habit of expecting her to carry him around. At ten months, he started speaking some words: "dada", "mummy", "pooh"; imitated his father saying "get out", and tried to say a girl's name, "Heia". He was never a happy child. He started walking at thirteen months. At eighteen months, playing hide-and-seek with his uncle, he was startled by his uncle appearing suddenly, and began to cry and laugh. From that moment his behaviour changed; he stopped speaking and wouldn't look at his mother or other people. He was very restless and kept walking all day long, moving his arms a lot, sometimes so he hit his ears. He was not interested in any toy, and looked like a puppet that walked and ate.

Whenever he was upset (for instance, when he was prevented from fiddling with the knobs of the cooker) he hit his head on the wall, turned round and round, opened and closed doors, and shook his body when he listened to music.

He became completely indifferent toward people and even at feeding time he made no contact with his mother. He developed an attachment to certain objects, holding them all day long. First there were cans, then a tape measure, the blender lid (he kept taking out and repositioning the small central cap), and magazines which he even slept with. That habit lasted until he was almost nine and, after that, he always kept his hands busy with something: fiddling with his shirt hem, buttons, etc.

At twenty-two months, he was taken to a neurologist, diagnosed as autistic and medicated. At thirty-eight months, when his brother was born, his parents noticed another change: "he began to revive", began to show a certain attachment to his brother, mother and father. He started trying to eat on his own, to communicate through gestures, and displayed a lot of concern with his brother who became "his own property". In that period, he insisted that his parents and brother were always together, even hand in hand, especially when the family was out of the house. He did not like, though, to be held on anyone's lap, or to be hugged or kissed.

He developed an interest in figures, letters and pointed at them for his mother to name them. It seemed that he already knew the names of the months, of the weekdays, colours and numbers up to 50. Yet he still didn't speak. He resumed speaking at five years and two months of age. At seven and a half, he started kindergarten. At eight and a half, he started attending a special school (CIAM) where he stayed until he started analysis. At that point his diction was still problematic, his buccal development very impaired. He had difficulty in cutting, painting, using a knife, etc. However he could read and write very well.

His sociability was "peripheral", he just watched other children play; he set himself apart and told stories in a sort of theatre of his own.

The preceding data, tests and other assessments were such that I began to see him four times a week, with the purpose of exploring his dynamic and structural condition.

The first sessions

When I first saw Mário, his demeanour was limp and disjointed. His eyes stared at me but seemed to droop, his mouth seemed unable to hold anything, his tongue was loose in his mouth, his arms and legs disjointed as if he were an uncoordinated puppet. His speech was an unmodulated drawl. He looked like a mentally disabled child, slow in making contact, who doesn't hear and doesn't understand. As soon as he entered the room, he asked me: "Is it already 3.15?" (the time for the appointment). He looked at me, smiled and sat down. He inspected the box and asked if he was going to stay until four o'clock and if he could play with the toys in the box. Then he got close to the box and started grabbing one toy at a time, naming them and saying: "Now I'm going to take the pencil, now the rubber, now…", and so on. After noting and naming everything, he put them back one by one in their place. He named the objects without using them, without giving them meaning, without connecting them.

In the following sessions, he enacted stories with the dolls, or would lay them aside and start performing in the middle of the room, standing up, gesturing, clapping his hands disjointedly and walking, like an actor speaking to the audience:

Mário: Everything began in prehistory. Their adventure began in prehistory. Then God created the world. Then Adam and Eve's time began. The old man was a ploughman and the old woman just cooked. Then Noah's time began. Then after that, the old man started another job. He had to collect fire, to make fire, as in prehistory. Then after that, Abraham's time began. Then the old man went back to being a ploughman of the earth. Then Jesus Christ's time began. And then Europe was discovered. Then that old man and that old woman spoke other languages like Portuguese, Spanish, Dutch, Swedish, French, English and Russian. Then the Ancient times began. Then the old man and the old woman wanted to have a baby that they'd never had, even in the time of prehistory. Then the old woman gave birth to a son. That boy lived a hundred years. Then he died and the old man and the old woman got very sad. And that's the end!" (*Pause.*) "And then began the times of other discoveries in Europe. The old man and the old woman spoke not only seven languages but started speaking other languages. Then the times of Independence began. Then the old man and the old woman started to have complete freedom. Then the time of the Republic began. Then the old man started being more polite and stopped abusing the old woman.

   Analyst: Why did he abuse her?
   Mário: Sometimes he abused her! And after that son they didn't have another child. (*Pause.*) I want to know everything that happened in 1966!
   Analyst: You want to know your story, the story of your birth.

It seems that he doesn't hear what I say and lies down warbling: "Who is the highest bidder for one John Doe… Who dares to believe a guy...".

He breaks wind and lies down until the end of the session.

Mário's storytelling-sequences – a step towards a relationship

As the analysis develops, the biblical voices yield to fables, radio performances, and sleeping during some parts of the session. On awaking Mário would seek for snug physical contact with the couch, the cushions and the walls. He would touch my shoes, grab my arm to see the time on my watch. I tell him that when he stops speaking in his speaker's voice, there emerges a small boy who feels many things here with me and doesn't know how to express them. He smiles, as if in answer. During his performances, he demands that I keep listening without interrupting, as if I'm someone in the audience. He gets restless, swinging arms and legs in movements similar to those of a puppet being set in motion by strings.

He would broadcast his "radio show", using up the whole session. I had to remain a controlled object, the prey of his words. It is hard to remain in that role, I feel useless and, when that feeling becomes intense, I react. This is what happens, for instance, in the session I describe below.

Session of May 4th, 1978 – "The interruption"

Mário enters the room, his face congested by a cold. I look him straight in the eyes to establish contact. He starts the usual series of singsongs in the middle of the room, facing the door and turning his back to me: "They say my friend is deaf… it seems absurd to be spanked so much… Tambourine, no, Bass Drum, that's my name – Tambourine doesn't eat, but can be spanked…".

Sitting on the chair, I realize I am expecting that Mário is going to do his usual performance, while I wait for him to contact me directly after he has finished. Then I become aware that he has tied me up in this expectation, and keeps all my sensuous attention occupied with his enactment. So I interrupt him, getting up and placing myself in front of him, in the middle of the room, saying that now I will tell him a story. He says not now, only after he's finished. I tell him it must be now, otherwise I will forget later, and, very reluctantly, he lets me begin, but next, lying down on the couch, he roars and hits with his fist, saying that we shouldn't do that then.

The story is that once upon a time there was a boy called Mário, who, when he met Dr Marisa, got so scared that, in an effort to feel better and more reassured, brought with him a long story to relate, which he already knew from start to end. And while he was telling that story, he could, hiding behind it, watch Dr Marisa and himself a little bit when they were together. Protesting violently, weeping, he lets me finish, as if I had spoiled his toy.

I stop speaking and he gets up to go on with his enactments. But he gets dizzy and leans on the wall. I get up saying that if he had listened to me, he would have noticed what is going on in him and couldn't pretend that everything remained the same. He is whining a bit, yelling a bit, trying to prevent me from continuing and saying that I have spoiled everything.

I tell him that he feels scared and unprotected as if I had taken a pacifier, teddy bear or little worn-out comforter away from him. That he feels that he can keep growing up here if I let him use his pacifier-performance. He resumes his usual play-enactment, but in another state of mind, with his face and eyes lively, keeping in touch with me through his look. I point out the change to him.

The session came to an end before he had finished the broadcast and he left still talking.

After that experience, I was moved to find another way to connect with him, interrupting him and pointing out to him the structure of the relationship he maintained with me, which consisted in "tying me up" with his storytelling sequences and preventing me from "interfering". Among his resources for maintaining that mode of relationship, he would establish a schedule for the entire session with the bombardment of his unremitting, sometimes very loud talking, enacting the characters as if in a theatre inside which he seemed to feel emotions apparently caused by the unfolding of his own stories. Another resource was an activity in which he named, grouped or made endless lists, from the beginning to the end of the session, an activity that I considered void of meaning and emotion. Confronted by these types of behaviour, I often felt I didn't have the tools to respond to him analytically, and my countertransference feelings, sometimes, were of discouragement, or even of a desire to get rid of that bombing. I tried to get closer to him, placing myself inside his stories, or enacting and verbalizing the role he assigned to me in the transference (baby, student, listener), but those were intermittent efforts that I soon relinquished, for his response was to ignore my presence, and I needed a response to move forward.

Little by little, it was established that I was the representative (in the transference) of a baby who had no place to stay, who couldn't be heard, who couldn't move, all alone, with no-one to rely on. That aspect in him of destitution and dereliction, and its counterpart, of a tyrannical reporter-commentator for that baby, now became very clear. Since the storytelling sequences he enacted were the defence mechanisms he resorted to in order to refrain from getting in touch with his mind when he was with me, it was unclear how to work through the non-contact and non-bonding situation that they covered. There were some escapes from it, in the form of gestures, touches, movements during the performances, which, like Freudian slips, could indicate unconscious elements showing through the gaps, produced by the transference relationship.

There were also, within the storytelling sequences, some flashes of apparent meaning. On the one hand, I thought it wasn't appropriate to pay attention to the contents, which were anyway very difficult to follow, and resulted in me in getting into the game of making out the meaning of his words. On the other hand, I questioned whether the best procedure was just to focus on the relationship structure of his defence and not to use the material he communicated during his stories.

The fact is that the material he communicated was very obscure to me, and I often thought it had the function of blocking me up. In addition, there was the difficulty of withstanding the sensorial bombing of his enactments – his loud and ceaseless talk. It was mainly the "escapes" during the enactments that gave me the chance to get in touch with the other Mário – the one who, for instance, while the speaker discussed the most recent world events, was clinging to a cushion, touched the room doors and his anus, displaying preoccupations very different from the commentator's. From time to time, there suddenly emerged verbalizations in his stories that seemed to allude to a current emotional state, to his life circumstances – such as, reference to "accident", or to his mental disorder.

I now turn to a session three months after the previous one I have related.

Session of September 13th, 1978 – "The bogeywoman"

Mário: Good afternoon. We're going to present "The Yellow Woodpecker Ranch",[i] in the series *The Bogeywoman Will Catch You,* and "The Start of the Saci Chase".[ii] Pete, Miss-Cute-Little-Nose, Emily and the Viscount went to Uncle Barnaby's home, and he told them the Saci story and asked if they were willing to chase the Saci. Then, they started chasing the Saci and called Short-Tail. Then, during the chase, Pete felt a wind so strong that it seemed like a hurricane. Then everybody fled and then they didn't have the courage to chase

---

i   The Yellow Woodpecker Ranch is the set for the children's books written by Brazilian writer Monteiro Lobato. In 1920 "The Girl with the Turned-up Nose" was the first of a series of twenty-three stories. The children's tales were turned into widely popular TV programmes including five series of the "Yellow" in the 50s, 60s, 70s and 2000. Several generations of Brazilian children have been thrilled and educated by these wonderful stories.

ii   The Saci is the most popular character in Brazilian folklore: a one-legged elf that smokes a pipe, he is able to appear and disappear as he wishes thanks to a magic red cap. He is considered to be an annoying prankster.

the Saci anymore, for more or less ten days. Now I'm going to present "Your Request is Worth Prizes." First request made by Sonia Regina, from Rio Bonito. It's the Saint-Exupéry ensemble "C'est la vie". (*He sings the song.*) Now, the last request: made by Claudio de Almeida Bastos from Santo Amaro. With Roberto Leal: "Maria's Country." (*He sings the song.*) Bye, guys! Talk to you next week!

He finishes and sits on the couch. There is a pause.

This is one of the moments when he allows space for some direct contact, sometimes for talking. The first part of the session, when he is performing, singing, I must keep quiet. I am the audience watching him, sitting at my place, and, little by little, while he tells stories, he is able to look at me, to watch me. This way, an aspect of his mind emerges, communicating through movements of the arms, eyes, when opening the cupboards, tapping the doors, etc., which all seem to be escaping from the performance that constitutes his defence.

The stories now have a structure, a sequence, logic, an evolution of content. Each time they are less chimerical and clearer. In the first part of the session, he "shoves me to a corner" in order to have a large space for himself. He seems to need to act this way, to keep his distance, and little by little (we aren't able to achieve it in every session) he gets closer, close enough for me to feel that I'm with someone in the room, to feel that I can hear him and he hears me, and both of us are aware of it. I am more able to follow his performances. Still, on countless occasions, I feel that I don't have anything to do in the context of the isolation in which he places me at those times. Many times, I try to get close by assuming one of the roles in the enactment game. Mário is always the narrator, the owner of the stories or the teacher of geography, history, etc.

I take an actual part in his performance, pretending to be the student who takes notes of what he is telling and repeating aloud what he is saying. My way of being with him is arguable, it's a probe planned to scrutinize his response and to know if it is useful to mark the boundaries of my presence in a material way. Maybe it would be more useful if I fought for room by trying to overcome feelings of helplessness brought on by that relationship.

To return to the session:

Mário pauses and sits down. He asks me to lend him *Veja*, a magazine belonging to the waiting room, saying that he will return it tomorrow. I ask him what he wants with a magazine for grownups. He says he likes to read the titles of the topics. I tell him that it's odd to like *Veja* at his age. Is it so he can feel like a grownup? Why?

He says that he can't read it, only the titles. It is as if he didn't eat food but just looked at it.

> **Analyst**: Tell me something that you like to eat.
> **Mário**: Apple.
> **Analyst**: So! Imagine that you think you've eaten an apple when, in reality, you have only stared at it?
> (*Mário is amazed and smiles.*)
> **Analyst**: So, if you don't get close to it, take it and bite, chew and swallow it, you don't take it inside. You don't get strong. You don't grow up.

Pause. He has listened to me all the time, sitting still, staring at me. Then, Mário plays a game. He takes the box of the Ludo board game which is next to him on the couch and says:

> **Mário**: I pretend that the box is a car. The car is in the garage. He had lunch and now the guys, the family went out. He went out. He was going to travel. (*He pushes the box up to the other end of the couch.*) Then the truck came and crash! Then the fire started and all the family died... he died. Then, the car wasn't useful anymore and was all torn to pieces. End of the accident story.

He returns the box to its place. Then, he takes the cushion and tries to squeeze it his arms and lips, licks and sucks it, spits on it, throws it away, on the floor. Now, with his feet on the wall, he keeps staring at me and stroking the wall.

Mário (cunningly): Will you lend me *Veja*?

Analyst (laughing): Oh yeah! For you to show at home that you are the person in charge of keeping my things!

Mário smiles and pushes my chair with his feet. End of the session.

Throughout the following months, Mário's stories showed content that sometimes seemed to be connected to the "here and now" of the analytical relationship and sometimes seemed to be an externalization of his "thoughts" about himself. I have selected some representative sessions.

Session of September 21st, 1978 – "The doctor who fooled people"

Mário: Pinocchio in "The doctor who fooled a lot of people." An old doctor was walking through the village when, all of a sudden, he ran into a man and said, "Why are you so sad?" "Because a wolf has eaten all of my hens and I don't have eggs to eat anymore." Doctor: "Don't worry, I'm crying for you." "Who are you, anyway?" "I'm Doctor Sadness. When I see sad people I cry for them, but I've got a remedy for that, the happiness remedy." The man takes the medicine. Then the doctor ran into a woman and said, "Why are you so sad? Oh! Why are you so sad?" "Because I left my home and now I don't have anywhere to go." Doctor: "Don't worry, I'm crying for you." And the doctor cried. Then the woman asked, "Who are you, anyway?" "I'm Doctor Sadness, but don't worry, I have the happiness remedy. Take it!"

Some time later, the doctor said, "The medicine is finished, I need to make some more. But first I need to find where I'm going to spend the night."

Then another day, Pinocchio met the raven laughing. Then all the village animals met together in a general meeting. "We have to choose someone able to solve the problem of the raven, the mole and the rabbit. It can only be Pinocchio. Because you are the one who understands the language of people and animals." "OK, I'll go", said Pinocchio. And he dozed off and broke the medicine bottle. Then the doctor forgave him and Pinocchio asked him to make a different remedy, "to turn me into a person. Will you make it?" The doctor makes it: "There. It's done." Pinocchio takes it, then laughs loudly. "Why doesn't the remedy work in me? Because I'm made of wood."

"Hey, Pinocchio! Aren't you going to solve the problem of the raven, the mole and the rabbit?" "Why are those guys laughing?" said Ladrinário. "Because they took the happiness remedy." "We don't believe it", Ladrinário yelled.

The phantasy that Mário is different from humans has begun to appear in his stories and comes up also in subsequent sessions: the psychoanalytic medicine does not help, the King-father wants to burn him for being strange, a being from another planet that may attack him once he is grown up. The Cardinal intervenes, advising the king that the puppet is sent from God and will free him. But the violin does not work and Pinocchio gives up on becoming a real boy because it is impossible to repair the damage – the only option is to make another boy.

Mário became upset during this dramatization and was unable to continue for a moment. I tell him he is feeling emotional. He denies it, claiming it was just a very long story.

Session of October 3rd, 1978 – "The xerox's truth"

I receive Mário 10 minutes earlier than usual. He will undergo EEG when he leaves this session.

Contact – he hits me with the cushion. He kicks the stool. He opens the cupboards. We fight. He is closer, more real, and not offish like yesterday when he called me a hypocrite. He says he is from Jupiter. He tries to bite my finger. I tell him that biting is something that happens on this planet. There is more fighting. He kicks me, hits me and I try to get a hold on him. He calms down.

He starts pretending that he is biting me, but on my whole body, on the chest and on the back.

Mário: Bad touching with the finger. You didn't give your finger and then he (*the being from the planet Jupiter*) will be forced to eat you up. And he left a xerox copy but you were in his belly. Then he left the tower and went to the primal planet. Getting there, the King said, "Where are the beings from the Earth?" And he answered, "They're in his belly." The King sent the being from the planet Jupiter to be shot. Then when he died, they saw – the King saw – that the guys from the Earth weren't there, it was just one human being, it was just you (*addressing me*). Then they went to Jupiter, no, to the Earth, disguised themselves as humans and carried the xerox to their planet and left the original here, which was you. Then, they went to Jupiter again and the King sent for the Scientist who made the xerox vanish because it wasn't useful anymore. It was like allowing his predecessor to go to Jupiter and his successor stayed there for a long time until he fell apart more and more and then... (*His speech gets very obscure.*) It happened to prevent the xeroxes of others being sent from Jupiter to Earth.

Analyst: Is that the idea that you have of here? That you come here to put my xerox inside you, to turn you into a person?

With a pen, he scratches concentric circles on the table to show me how the xerox falls apart.

Mário: You have to cut the xerox in half. That is the xerox's truth.

I will also give here an illustrative passage from another session approximately three months after this one:

Mário lies down still. He stares at me a lot. I tell him that he would like to talk to me. He turns on the fan, fiddles, I warn him not to turn on the heat – he obeys. After a while, he starts whispering: "I don't understand." I ask him what he doesn't understand, but he seems not a bit concerned whether I follow him or not. He keeps talking: "Whoever has a thinking mind goes to Cuba…Whoever has a rising sun mind goes to Argentina…Whoever has a magician's mind goes to New York", etc.

I say: "Whoever has a Dr Marisa mind goes on vacation. Whoever has a Dr Marisa mind goes where she pleases." He laughs but goes on for a little while. Then he stops, kicks the floor and the wall, scratching it with his shoe.

I tell him that this is a way of talking to me.

Still lying down, he starts again, with a mute performance, just with his body and sounds, communicating the idea of something moving towards bursting point. I tell him that he makes things up, imagines everything inside the room, while I see a boy who finds it very difficult to talk to me.

It doesn't take much to demonstrate to the reader how all my various interventions were attempts (to the point of exhaustion) to search for meanings in Mário's conduct which could open gaps for me to go beyond his defence mechanisms and to make contact with his buried baby-self, in order to achieve a more vital communication and relationship. By then I was already convinced that merely pointing out the way to relate to me wasn't enough.

We have already noted in this first chapter that his stories began as biblical voices and then began to contain more specific allusions to his own condition, his fantasies about his derangement and the causes of his disorder. These began in the series "Pinocchio and the doctor who fooled a lot of people", "The miraculous violin", "God's son", or "The xerox's truth". While in other stories, the emotional situation present in his relationship with me was more obvious, as for instance in the "Diary of a lonely man" or "The bogeywoman will catch you" sessions.

The Third Semester of the Analysis – 1979

Returning after the vacation, Mário displayed an intensification of his defence mechanisms. He spoke like some poets who improvise in the street, as in "Analysis of the Second World War" and "Analysis of Getulio Vargas' death." He whispered, lying down on the couch. He was very resentful of schedule changes that had to be made because of his school needs and for his mother's convenience. During that period, in February 1979, he often talked about borders between the States. I tell him that this way he gets reassured that he knows where he ends and the analyst starts, a need that may have emerged from the time we spent apart during the summer vacations. Finally, he talks about his State and what there is in his State: "There are foreign relations, animals, people etc.", and he finishes with: "in my State there's death."

In another session, he talks about friends and classmates who had died: one in an accident, another from a heart attack, one run down by a car, one drowned, a girl was murdered, and only Mário and Silvio remained. He spends the time lain down, making lists while the body moves with his feet on the wall, kicking the power outlet. Standing up, he turns the fan on and off, the light switch, opens and closes the cupboards in the room. Such behaviour seems to express that he's taking possession and controlling the room-analyst-object.

However, he gradually comes to express more directly his resentment at having been left behind during the holidays, whilst denying his dependence, as in the following session.

Session of February 12th, 1979 – "I want to be your friend again"

Mário greets me and sits down. His feet are muddy and stain the floor and the couch. He lies down and leans his feet on the wall and touches the power outlets. He says: "In this year, 1979, will I come to therapy just once? Or will I come four times a week, as I did in 1978? Monday, Tuesday, Wednesday and Thursday?" I listen carefully, trying to find out what he wants to express.

Mário: It's because it's everyday, everyday! Now I'm not in that class at school any more. And because I leave before the others, I can't go to English and electronics. And no-one knows where I go. I don't have time to tell them that I come to therapy.

Analyst: Hum!

Mário: Well, Miss Marisa? Don't you think that once a week is enough? It's impossible not to make any other appointments when every day I have to come here and, when it gets to Friday, I'm worn out and don't want to go anywhere.

Now he begins to define his complaint better. It's a sacrifice to come here. He continues:

Mário: And it's far! Full of trucks and buses! A fucking truck was in front of us spouting fumes! Eh! I'm tired of being an amateur runner (anonymous).

I say that he is complaining about me, that I force him to come here and that he comes because of me. He is still lying down, facing me, talking to me, and now he turns around so that he won't see me or hear me.

Mário: And now I have to listen to this stuff, these... these... What you say is deniable... comes from philosophy, doesn't it? Useless... psychoanalysis comes from a German philosopher, you know... and it isn't even accepted. I think that in Spain... it's nonsense! It's stupid!... It's...

I listen to him, amazed with his development, and tell him that the fact that he had come so many times last year is now proving its usefulness in helping him say what he thinks about me and the analysis.

Mário: Enough! You are giving off oil, spouting fumes... (*Sound of loud bangs outside.*)

Analyst: Like those trucks outside?

Mário: You should be behind bars.

Analyst: That's what you think you need in order to feel that you control me. What distresses you is that I'm not you, but you need me – and I'm not here and turn into bad fumes that you have to get rid of.

He starts spitting, kicks things in the room, punches and hits me, then emits loud roaring sounds from the centre of his mouth: "Mummy, Mummy, Mu…" and I follow him repeating the sounds: "kika, ba, bo…". I say that the "baby-mummy" is furious.

He lies down, seems empty. I say that he's waiting for all of his "mummies", "kikas" to leave his mouth, that he feels like an empty bag, but he can see that I am here.

After a pause, he stands up and says: "Dr Marisa, I want to be your friend again, let's be friends." And he reaches out his hand. I say that he destroyed me inside him, but that he was able to fix it when he noticed that I stayed here with him. The session ends and, before leaving, he cleans up all the muddy stains.

On his return from the holidays, Mário's obsessive defences intensified over the course of several weeks. I will give the notes of another session from this period that may help to convey Mário's own awareness or view of his perturbation:

Session of March 19th, 1979

When I go to call Mário I tell his mother that I shall not be working the next Thursday. She says the neuro-paediatrician wants to talk to me, that Mário has been aggressive and he thinks that it might get out of control and then he would have to increase the medication. I propose an appointment to talk to the parents. The mother agrees. When we get in, Mário, whose face is marked by smudges of merthiolate (antiseptic), sits on my chair – something he has been doing for several recent sessions – and begins a performance in which he is a mythology teacher. He speaks incomprehensibly most of the time. When he finishes, he gets up and there is a crisis of loss of control, during which he physically assaults me and I have to hold him firmly. After this acting-out episode is over, he leaves my chair and sits on the couch.

He goes on to talk about a treasure that is hidden and must be found and he is the main character. I tell him that people are complaining that he is being aggressive and that he is losing control like a boy without intelligence. But that he was able to get his parents to come to me so that I could explain what is really happening to him. That he must learn to express himself, and not be forcibly restrained, but be understood.

He maintains the attitude of someone who is not listening. I get up and tell him that I want to talk to him. He says: "You've already said some of it." I say it is hard to know whether he is listening or not. He listens and after a pause approaches me, takes my wrist, and – looking at the middle of the room, where there is a rug – tells me to put the dots on the U, two dots on the U, like this: Ü (he writes it on a piece of paper) and goes on: "Over there is the sea (the rug), inside there is a house (and I ask whether it is submerged and he answers affirmatively), inside it there is a dog, inside the dog there is a cat, inside the cat there is a mouse, and inside the mouse is a piece of cheese. You cut the cheese in the middle and you have the U with the two dots: Ü. Then you divide it and there is just one dot: Û. I lost this dot. This is the treasure that must be found and you are going to help me find it!"

I say that it must be just there inside him.

Comments by Donald Meltzer and Martha Harris

In August 1979, when Donald Meltzer and Martha Harris visited the Brazilian Psychoanalytic Society in São Paulo, I showed them the four sessions recounted above: "The interruption", "The bogeywoman", Pinocchio in "The doctor fooled a lot of people", "The xerox", and "I want to be your friend again."

Donald Meltzer and Martha Harris made the following comments on these sessions:

The stories may be verbalizations about his mental state when he left. They are autistic objects to which he is addicted and a defence against thought and emotions. When he presents his adult side (the puppet), the baby vanishes from view. However, the stories are important as a means of communication and from them one is able to extract material in order to communicate with him. It is necessary to look for moments in the session when the young and frightened child is present, in order to interpret. But it is necessary to interrupt him when the analyst has something to say. He is connected to the analyst like a containing skin. And he identifies that what he needs is the equipment used by the analyst in order to think. He utilizes adhesive identification, protecting himself from feeling detached every time that he doesn't have an internal object. It demonstrates the difficulty that the autistic child has in shaping a tri-dimensional object which allows introjection and projection.

At this point they mentioned the book *Explorations in Autism* (Meltzer et al., 1975), which I was not previously aware of, explaining that it was written after a ten-year collaboration between a group of therapists from Tavistock under Meltzer's supervision, in order to deepen knowledge of the autistic mind and the post-autistic organization.

For a young analyst completing her training at the São Paulo Institute, taking on the analysis of a boy with these behavioural patterns was a challenge. One may observe in that first period my attempts to establish contact with Mário as if he were a child with neurotic defences. The supervision of Dr Vida Maberino de Prego helped me to understand the nature of his obsessive defences, the search for deceptive coverings and confusions in order to hide what is really worthy, and the pubertal changes taking place in a personality whose emotional development had suffered an interruption.

One may notice, however, by means of fragments of my notes, that Mário's externalizing faced me with the sense of an enigma that must be disclosed at each session. Quite often I could follow the transference aspects of the situation, or features of his stories that seemed to communicate disguisedly what he wanted to say directly. But Mário's baby-self appeared in the pre-verbal language. The verbal language was used to oppress the baby-self who, in the transference, was the analyst.

I felt poorly equipped to understand his personality structure and functioning, and Dr Meltzer's and Martha Harris' supervision in August 1979 paved the way for me to get acquainted with the most recent studies in autism. That contact was continued through supervisions both by mail and in my trips to London, enabling me to keep Mário's analytical process going. The second chapter will illustrate that change of course in my work with Mário.

CHAPTER TWO

Applying the post-Kleinian understanding of autistic states

During the analysis' fourth semester I started to get acquainted with the picture of autistic mental structure arrived at by Meltzer in *Explorations in Autism* (1975). I began to see things going on in the consulting room that I had never seen before. Although Meltzer stated that the analytical technique to analyse children like Mário was the same as with other children, in the beginning I found it difficult to situate myself within the very deep comprehension of the ongoing analytical process that this entailed. My difficulties I believe resulted from a training still insufficiently equipped to make use in the clinic of the concepts introduced by Melanie Klein and extensively taught and often improved by Meltzer himself.

The clinical work with autistic children undertaken by the group of Kleinian psychoanalysts under the supervision of Donald Meltzer in *Explorations* resulted in proposing the following modalities of mental functioning in autistic children: a special kind of dissociation that Meltzer called "dismantling", a notable difficulty with the categories of space and time, an archaic use of the obsessive mechanisms, and the phenomenon of mindlessness that can be viewed as an extreme case of dismantling.

This concept of the autistic disorder arose from psycho-analytic examination of the transference, and it attained an important indirect corroboration when studying dismantling in post-autistic states. Autism is a kind of retardation of develop-ment that tends to occur in some very intelligent children with a high degree of emotional sensitivity in the context of a mother figure who is suffering from depressive states during their first year of life. This leads them into intense depressive anxieties at the very time when the maternal figure is unable to provide the care needed to share and modify "this deluge of mental suffering".

Given an obsessive predisposition, the response to the object deprivation may be drastic; that is, it can lead to trying to deal with anxiety through fantasies of the omnipotent control of objects. These children employ a dissociation mechanism with which they dismantle their ego into separate perceptive capaci-ties: touch, smell, etc., as a result of which the object, instead of having a "common sense" (Bion), is reduced to a multiplicity of mono-sensual events in which animate and inanimate aspects are indistinguishable.

The oscillation in experiencing the "common sense" object and the experience of the dismantled object, added to the factor of the mother's unavailability, interferes in the evolution of the concept of internal space not only in the self, but also in the object, thus impoverishing the processes of introjection and projection. Consequently, the ego tends to remain in a primi-tive state of fusion with its external object through a fantasy of adherence (Bick), resulting in a highly narcissistic form of identification, which heightens intolerance to separation. The primitive nature of the ego, the characteristic anxieties, and the oscillation between autistic and integrated conditions, create a very confusing picture.

As the patients recover or improve, this picture is replaced by another: a mix of immaturity and obsessive traits. This is the setting for the occurrences through which we can understand mutism.

The difficulty in the processes of introjection deriving from the failure in forming the concept of internal space favours a failure in language development, because the processes of identification with speaking objects are arrested. Adhesive narcissistic identification stimulates identification with body object functions over mental ones. And later, when introjection and projection are more functional, pre-genital Oedipal jealousy interferes in the verbal intercourse of internal objects, leaving them separate and silent. This is in addition to the tendency for non-vocalization, even if the internal language is developing.

The impoverished identifications and the dehumanized aspects of the objects do not stimulate the desire to communicate; they only reinforce the wish to disobey or provoke obedience in the objects, for which purpose gestures and signs are enough.

I will now relate some of the sessions with Mário that took place when, with the help of Meltzer's supervisions (postal and in person), I began to apply my increased understanding of the Kleinian model of the structure of post-autistic states.

Session of August 15th, 1979

From the moment of entry Mário appears in an agitated condition. He talks in a very loud voice. He is relating a story about a werewolf who, on waking up, has to take certain measures before the full moon wanes. I intervene many times to tell him how I found him distressed, and fearful of being with me. He does not let me talk, does not stop to listen to me, and continues the story almost shouting. The atmosphere is extremely fraught and charged with emotion.

Mário: No, mother! I don't want to go the castle! I don't want to, no mother! (*Nobody replies. He looks down at the floor.*) Funny! First it was Joseph, then Simon, then Nestari. And now Datale? I'm going to investigate! (*He turns his back.*) Wow – ow – ow – ow!... Ah! Ah! Ah! (*Diabolical shrieks of laughter.*) Fall into the trap.

I say that he is telling a story in which anyone wanting to know something falls into a trap, and this trap swallows up the person and makes them disappear; it wakes up the werewolf within himself which threatens him greatly.

He continues his story by talking to an imaginary hole in the floor. Again, anyone who ventures to look in is just one more who falls into the trap and disappears. And he finishes by saying "and they were thrown into the tunnel which goes to the centre of the earth… Mother! Mother!" he calls repeatedly (and there is no reply).

I tell him that he is alone; his mother doesn't reply; he is himself this werewolf, throwing himself into a hole in the earth and nobody can do anything, not even me who is here with him.

End of session.

Meltzer's comment: This kind of material may be seen as referring to the confusion between the top and bottom of the maternal body, between a bleeding vagina from which father's penis has been withdrawn, a bleeding breast from which the nipple has been bitten off. In either case the hole, as an object of persecutory depression, sucks the child in a projective identification as a defence against the depressive pain and produces a state of mind like been lost inside a haunted and sinister castle.

Session of August 16th, 1979

Mário arrives five minutes late, holds out his hand, asks me if he is late, then leads me to my chair for me to be seated. He seems less distressed. He continues his story about the werewolf, saying that it has been captured; the gold had been found and the stolen objects recovered.

Today he is alright with me, with no threats, and a friendly communication is re-established between us.

He goes to the bookshelf where he knows there are some old magazines. He separates those which have dates from those without dates. He takes them all and puts them on top of the table. Then takes them all back to the bookshelf, putting those without dates on top. He chooses one of the magazines called *Manchete* ("Headline") and turns over the pages numerous times.

I tell him that by looking and looking at the same magazine he is making sure that nothing new or surprising has missed him. He then tucks the magazine under his arm and asks to go to the toilet. In there he talks and on returning to the room continues talking: "Aries (*the ram*) is from the second half of March to the second half of April. Tauro (*the bull*) is from the second half of April to the second half of May…" (and he continues with the signs of the Zodiac).

I tell him that he is playing tricks by joining the toilet and the room, talking both outside in the toilet and here inside the room, in order to give his talking a continuous sequence, owing to his fear and distress at having to leave here today and not come back until after the weekend.

Meltzer's comment: Here you see the child recovered from his nightmare of projective identification and relating himself both to the top (bookcase) and the bottom (toilet) of the analytic mother. He is trying to put some order into his confusion of how these two parts are related to each other in time and space. The magazine represents what he introjects from the feed and which he fears to lose, falling out of him when he is toileting. The signs of the Zodiac represent the part-object – penis and nipple – which put order into the time and space of his relation to the mother.

After this supervision it became clear that my way of talking to Mário was not getting to the level of the psychic organization in which he was moving. Thus, when I said to him that the knowledge frightened him, it threatened him like a werewolf. I wanted to address an aspect of him that could contain the impulse toward knowledge and the fear of it.

But Meltzer's comment opened out a much more primitive level of organization that corresponded to his experiencing a third person's presence as an invasion, with imminent catastrophe due to the emotions of possessiveness and jealousy that made him "pull out the breast nipple", viewing it as an intruder, and re-establish the mutual mother–baby idealization.

Later, when I re-read the material of the sessions I had sent to Meltzer for supervision, together with his comments, I would review the material from the previous sessions as a kind of exercise, in order to apply this new understanding in retrospect. The notes for the session two days before the one just recounted were as follows:

Session of August 14th, 1979

Mário knocked insistently on the door to come in. I was still tidying the room after the previous patient. He started dramatizing a radio broadcast singing romantic songs.

I told him that he seemed anxious to meet me and now "he was leaving me" (the song). He continued with the news broadcast: "The traffic is jammed between such and such streets. There is a crash between two cars."

I said that he seemed not to hear me but the mental traffic was jammed by my presence, there were crashes.

He continued talking and did not stop to listen to me; soon after he was talking about the strangulation of adulterous couples in Iran, etc. He went on: "And now the investigation of the very act."

The material of this session seems to display fantasies of crashes (between him and me), the strangulation of adulterous couples (me and the previous patient, whom he might have seen), and an investigation of the very act (me busy preparing the room); but these connections were made by me only after the session.

After Meltzer's supervisions, my view of what was going on in these sessions was that Mário's insistence on getting into the room showed partly his idea of his prerogative – that it was *his* appointment – but more than that, the fact that, hearing the sound of the room being put in order, he could not bear to wait without seeing what was going on. When he saw me, this reassured him, and he could assume the role of daddy-partner in face of mummy-Marisa as shown by singing romantic songs. When I pointed out that he was not really listening to me, it is possible that he momentarily became aware of his failure of real contact, by contrast with the imaginary contact. As the session progressed, the possible motives for evading actual contact became clearer: the fantasies of crashes, strangulation, etc., that he possibly had while knocking insistently on the door to get in.

In the session of August 15th, when he had arrived very agitated, ready to be thrown into a hole in the centre of the earth (the hole produced by pulling the nipple-penis from the breast), he had separated the combined nipple-breast (or penis-vagina) object owing to his possessiveness and Oedipal jealousy. And the next day (August 16th) he showed a manic reparation, re-establishing control through a mutual idealization of mother and baby.

Correspondence with Dr Meltzer

I will transcribe here some questions and answers from my postal correspondence with Dr Meltzer regarding this period in Mário's analysis.

1) I experiment in being more of an interventionist; I interrupt him so that I do not remain, let's say, in the place where he puts me in the transference. He responds to his change of mine with a more direct contact, but resulting in aggression on some occasions.

Meltzer's comment: This will present him with a more combined-object experience with you (breast and nipple, top-and bottom-combined, mother and father), both reassuring but also arousing Oedipal feelings.

2) A different dramatization: Mário places my chair on the floor and puts a stool between his legs. He says, "There is the

invisible Marisa." I say, "And the invisible Mário placed himself between the invisible Marisa."

Meltzer's comment: The mother he never sees in intercourse with the father – his wish to be the penis that joins them together.

3) When he opens a cupboard, which he frequently does, underneath the washbasin, I ask him, "Is there anyone there? Invisible?" He said: "I am here, by the door."

Meltzer's comment: And to become the baby which the father puts into the mother.

4) A sequence of movements: Mário turns on the ventilator, the light, turns on the washbasin tap, opens the cupboards. From there he reverses the procedure, putting everything back in its place. He is careful to make sure that the reverse procedure is exact in every detail.

Meltzer's comment: A counter-Oedipal move – to make time reversible. This represents a manic reparation to the mother that results in the father becoming redundant. A basis for mutual idealization in the mother–baby relationship.

5) Other characteristics: Mário fills the basin with until the basin almost overflows, and then shuts the tap just in time. He carefully puts in his hand to make out the stopper, and watching the basin empty itself. He repeats the operation two or three times.

Meltzer's comment: Similar to the session of August 16th – monitoring the introjection and evacuation of mind and body.

6) The set of pens: once, some time ago, when playing, we hit upon a game to guess what the colours were, because some of the caps of the pens had been changed round. But today he changes all the caps, and begins the game by saying: "This pen with a brown cap – what is its true colour?" But, in presenting the pen, he had looked at the base and seen its colour. I tell him that in that way I too can guess because I'm watching. But he doesn't think this important. What is important to him is that he can

put the question, and that I give the reply expected by him. In other words I should reply that "It's real colour is green."

He insists, and gets angry if I don't reply as he wants me to. I point out that in this way, there are no disagreements either during the session or between one session and another.

When he detaches himself even more, talking of sports programmes to an imaginary public, he makes me into a real representative of this public; he is in contact with me, sees me in the room, looks at me, watches how I am, but is very busy with this programme. I say, "Mário! What's become of you? Where are you?" He gives me an expressive look – a lively look by comparison with the veiled and stony looks given on former occasions. I say, "The sequence describes Mário's mother. Mário will not be alone. The mother-sequence is here to accompany you."

Meltzer's comment: A game to guess the part which creates the confusion between nipple – penis – anus – milk – faeces - good – bad, etc. It implies an x-ray eye looking inside the object. It reveals the paranoid element of his personality, that there is a part of the self mixed up with an object that creates confusion (Bion in *Attention and Interpretation*: the creator of lies, the negative grid, the delusional system.) The "commentator" who interferes with observation and thought by imposing his own perverse judgement on everything above all claims to see and understand the primal scene. The know-it-all part.

The fourth semester of analysis, October to November 1979

This was the period in which the difficulties in speaking and being heard were accentuated, because I started to give more significance to it and this disturbed Mário's defensive set-up and shattered his omnipotent control. There was almost no room for me, he occupied the space all the time; I started to speak loudly next to him and this caused an aggressive reaction, even physically, with the aim of shutting me up. As Meltzer explained, this omnipotent control and separation of objects was a defence against Oedipal feelings: he was both the penis and the baby inside the mother. I saw that either I spoke or he spoke according to his plan of making sure there was no "contamination", intent on keeping well separated what is his from what is mine. Whenever I interrupted this scheme of things his plan was disturbed, and this opened cracks in which where Oedipal feelings might appear.

When he felt too threatened by these Oedipal feelings, he would develop a counter-move, by making time reversible and by manic reparation of the mother. This showed itself in the room in various ways. For instance, he might switch on the fan, turn on the light, the washbasin tap, or open up the cupboards. Then he would do the reverse: shut the cupboards, turn off the tap, turn off the light and the fan. In these instances the move is made on the level of the parts of the room representing the parts of the body of the Marisa-mother.

Another counter-Oedipal move on the level of verbalization was, for example, to cite a list of figures or dates backwards. In this case the father became redundant and a base was laid for the mutual idealization of the mother–baby relationship.

When Mário is carried away during his talking to the "audience", he is turning me into its representative and, like a commentator-actor who knows it all, he prevents the Mário-baby from having contact with the breast-Marisa, or says that he himself is the breast. This is the reversion: he changes me into a baby that does not know the difference between good and bad, milk and urine, and he continues to present himself as a nipple pouring urine into my mouth-ear until my capacity of thinking is destroyed and I become his slave.

In this period of analysis Mário tells stories of explorations and Bible stories. It would be easy to explain to him the content of these stories, but the question which primarily presents itself is that it seems to me that the position he takes as a relator of stories is more important than their content. This is his way of playing, in which I have to take the part of the public or spectator, with him standing in the middle of the room. When I talk to or prompt him it is as awkward as it would be in a theatre if a member of the audience interrupted an actor on the stage. He really seems not to hear me, doesn't repeat any word which I have not caught: in short, in his pre-established role, any intervention of mine will interrupt the play. I assume that in all this he is realizing his dreams of being an actor, a speaker, a teacher, an important radio presenter, etc.

Is it simply a defence or is it a way for him to be able to develop an experience with me, if I can accept his "creations"? When this playacting is interrupted by me, or he spontaneously terminates his playacting, there is a more direct contact with me; physical attacks have occurred, or playing with other things in the room. So, during this period, I made an experimental approach of trying to "get inside" his game together with him. For example, when he told a story in which he assumed the role of a teacher or of a father, I would take on a complementary role.

Meltzer's comment: This is potentially endless confabulated pseudo-biblical time-wasting by the commentator and its content is not worth of attention, similar to Bion's concept of beta-screen. He has changed you into a baby who does not know the difference between good and bad. Milk and urine are mixed up (like the coloured pens), and he will continue to present himself as the nipple and urinate into your ear-mouth until your capacity to think has been killed by his insidious poison (propaganda) and you have become his slave.

I will give another example from this period: in October 1979 Mário commenced a story called "The treasure of Lumba-Lumba." Here two characters in the story find the treasure. When they open it is empty. "What's wrong! When we dug it out it was full!" A third voice says, "It was easy to hide the treasure inside my trousers. Ha! Ha! Ha! Ha!" Another voice says, "The treasure disappeared – it was a gorilla." I have the impression that he is hallucinated; from the movements he makes with his body the treasure has really disappeared and, moreover, there is a gorilla in the room. I wait quietly for him to give me "permission" to come in.

Meltzer's comment: The nipple has been removed and replaced by the penis of the bad part. The strategic operation is to expound the structure of the transference, how the gorilla-commentator usurps the position of the nipple between mother and baby, just is the boy-part would like to usurp the position of penis between mother and father in intercourse. It is necessary to "speak to" other parts of him (baby, boy, girl) to reclaim the usurpation of the relationship by the gorilla-actor. The massive interference must be broken through to re-establish the kind of contact that we have seen before.

Session of October 22nd, 1979

Mário comes in, looking at me, says "Let's continue", and opens the box to get pen and paper for me.

Mário: So Saul armed his servants and they all went to the lands of the kings of the Orient. At the same time the soldier who had delivered the letter to Saul was taken prisoner and put to death. Then Saul arrived on the opposite bank of the River Jordan. The battle began and was won by Saul's servants. One of the kings of the Orient liberated Ely and his servants, and so Saul, Ely and the servants all went away. God made Rebecca productive, and she will have a son who will be called Jordan.

In this session contact with me is much more direct – I get some response from him – and he suggests that I write his story down. His body moves in jerks like a puppet but, whilst swinging his arms about, he is at the same time holding a cushion that he has taken from the settee. He looks at me the whole time and turns almost to face me when I speak (rather than sideways or with his back turned as he does frequently). At one point in the session I stop writing and he insists that I continue to write. It was a moment when I was trying to stop playing in order to think about the actual game and its significance. Faced with his insistence that I continue writing, I tell him that I must have my mind free to think about him and that, at times, I cannot be tied to his dictation.

He freezes contact with me. He just doesn't reply when I ask him something I don't understand, and when I point out that in the content of the story he is telling there is ingratitude, wrath, destruction.

His face becomes more serious, he moves away from me and continues to hang on to the cushion. I tell him everything that I have been observing but he gives no sign of listening to me. I say that with his story of destruction, he felt he was being attacked by me when I stopped playing with him in order to think about him.

He then continues the story:

Mário: Now there is one who cried a lot, got influenza and died. At that moment Jonathan was born and there were festivities. When the festivities ended God said: "Saul, in ten years time you will go to Mount Orel when I will test you with Jonathan and a sheep. If you kill the sheep…" (*etc.*).

End of session.

Meltzer's comment: This commentator-actor-know-it-all prevents the baby from having contact with the breast as it claims to be the nipple itself. The gorilla reappears when the commentator is not obeyed! The dilemma between the gorilla who steals the breast and being the baby who wants it. Crucial! A reference to the story of Abrahan and Isaac – the problem of weaning (see *Fear and Trembling* – Kierkegaard).

Session of October 23rd, 1979

Mário commences by saying: "There is nothing I have to speak about so let's sing."

Analyst: But now it is my turn to speak. So Mário has now told a very important story. The story of his birth, of his life, of his brother's birth which left him feeling very abandoned with nowhere to go…".

He begins to switch on the light, then fills the hand-basin to the brim, then removes the stopper and empties the basin.

Analyst: Mário tries to close a hole which was in him when mother was expecting a baby and he felt shunned. The hate he felt was so great that he cannot believe in or like his mother anymore. So he stays by himself playing with his faeces, believing that by doing so he will grow up. But then Mário begins to see that needs his mother, his father, Marisa, and that it doesn't do to remain locked up in himself.

He begins to imitate me, saying "bla… bla… bla…".

Meltzer's comment: It is probably better to educate this transference first and then, if you wish, to trace its significance in the genetic dimension (reconstruction).

Analyst: So, Mário no longer likes what Marisa is saying. He thinks everything about people is very despicable. Yet perhaps Mário would be very upset if he could see that he and I are not two stories, nor two characters, nor two books, but just two persons.

He continues with a certain amount of "bla… bla…" as he does when he thinks what I'm saying is a lot of nonsense.

Then he recommences his story.

Mário: Solomon! Bala is sterile – marry Rachel… (*and so on*).

Meltzer's comment: A game from the gorilla-commentator. The beta-screen fills the baby with fears for the death the breast (weaning).

When the session finishes he makes for the door (as always shaking my hand on leaving), and says to me: "You great big fool and ass! I'll kill you."

Meltzer's comment: The gorilla!

Session of October 24th, 1979

As soon as Mário arrives he has a story ready to tell about a broken-down car which cannot be mended, not even by the Italians. I tell him to sit down, facing me; and remind him that yesterday he said that I was a great big fool and an ass, and that he would kill me. He says: "I have a plan." Then he begins to sing: "Bull, bull, black faced bull. Catch the girl who's afraid of a mask." Then he said the Italians were able to do the repairs, but were interrupted by bandits who said

"I'm going to kill that old man. Forget him and let's carry out our plan."

Meltzer's comment: Yes, the gorilla's claim that it can take on repairing that the daddy can do of the mummy, or that the breast can do of the baby's internal world.

I pointed out that there were those who mended, and those who broke things. In this session, Mário becomes increasingly excited and begins to roar in burst of fear, contempt, apparent madness. Not a moment of contact is possible; he is no longer listening to me at all.

Meltzer's comment: He is in a state of complete confusion of identity between good and baby parts of himself.

Then he stops. I take a sheet pf paper. He writes a heading and writes down numbers. It is a sequence starting with 5,000 and goes on decreasing. He is very much absorbed in what he is doing.

Meltzer's comment: Trying to put order into the chaos, as in the "Zodiac material".

Analyst: I don't exist for you right now. (A pause.) Can I look?
Mário: (shaking his head) No!
Analyst: (reading) "ANTIQUITY." Is this really what you wrote?
Mário: It is.

Analyst: Antiquity is a trick of yours. You are locking yourself up in your sequence of numbers. In that way you control yourself. You become very frightened when you become emotional here, as you did a little while ago. Frightened of being unable to control yourself?

Meltzer's comment: Yes, frightened of being confused in his identity.

Mário continues the orderly decreasing of numbers. It looks like a regression to the starting point – to the womb? to impregnation, the beginning of life, and being born again? Why?

Meltzer's comment: To regress to manic-reparation, running backwards to re-establish the mutual idealization of mother and baby with daddy not needed.

Analyst: You can't bear to see yourself as you are? A youth of thirteen years of age coming to analysis, and not recognizing what he is? You are not a god, not a floorboard, not a rattletrap and not a baby. (*All expressions used by him in former sessions.*)

He listens and, putting out his tongue, mutters "babababa-babababa, mamamamama!"

Meltzer's comment: The gorilla and the baby, alternating but distinguished from each other.

Session of October 25th, 1979

Mário continues the orderly decreasing of numbers until he finishes the page.
    Analyst: Have you finished?
    Mário: I've finished.
    Analyst: What have you finished?
    Mário: This job.
    Analyst: You've got to finish the sequence to be certain that it is in order. So that you can be free of this stuff in my presence.
    He lies down, appears empty-minded, with no programme.
    Mário: We are in a prison. In Aruana both Mário and Silvio are prisoners because they frightened a housemaid.

I tell him that he is still playing with his faeces-story. His corporal movements are more human, like a restless child, by contrast with the stiff and disconnected movements of a puppet. I point this out: there is now a boy present here. He continues with associations and sings "Black-faced bull" (a Brazilian lullaby) until, rising up, he looks at me and says: "Great big fool, I'm going to kill you."

He picks up a pen, goes to the middle of the room and throws the pen in my face. Then he gets on to the table and kicks me. I defend myself. We struggle.

Meltzer's comment: The experience of ambivalence, it is messy to become more in contact with his feminine side (the girl who is afraid of a mask).

Mário: I'm going to kill you. I'm not going to stop.

Analyst: The giant you wish to kill and whom you hate is reality. It is everything which isn't you; it's me and everything around you. Mário! You can't accept that you have already been born and lived thirteen years outside the womb, and think only of returning there?

He picks up the settee mattress and rolls it around him like a shield for protection against me (he's already done this during a previous session). I have to defend myself from being bumped whilst he goes rolling over and over on the floor. And there he remains, rolled up completely in the mattress on the floor, with me holding it.

Meltzer's comment: The wish to escape depression due to this ambivalence by going into projective identification (the maternal castle).

The session is over and, on leaving the room, he says, "I have not stopped yet; I'm going to try again; I will kill you." I say that his words lack conviction.

Session of November 19th, 1979 – Monday

He opens the box and then shuts it again. He sits on the settee.

Mário: Hi, so you didn't see that the oil of my car needs changing. Let's go, then? (*Enacting a continuation of one of his stories.*)

Analyst: We're here for whatever you need.

He seems not to listen and continues talking.

Mário: It's necessary to take out everything that's in the deposit.

Meltzer's comment: Back to the breast of August 16th.

Mário gets up, asks me to push the little basin towards him; he stands on it and opens the magazine cupboard and begins to take them out, one by one, reads the date of each then throws it on the table. After taking them all out he closes the cupboard. He sits down again on the settee and addresses me directly.

Mário: You can read them – the magazines are there.

Analyst: While taking the magazines out of the cupboard you are waiting to examine everything I have inside myself and to assure you what these things mean to you.

He now wants me to look inside me (the things on the table) – why? As a way of observing what is going on now in himself?

Meltzer's comment: This is the problem of being able to preserve the object in time, internally, of it turning to faeces and dropping out of his bottom (August 16th). The problem of preserving the object becomes once more an internal one, having been externalized for three months.

Mário is silent. Then he begins to talk about a church which, in 1964, had almost nothing in the way of furniture or paint-work. And, in 1971, it was painted but there was no furniture. I tell him that this describes his own state of mind, also talking of his birth, and how his parents made him. He goes on to talk of students who graduated in 1968 and of those who were in such and such a year and graduated in 1970. Then he stops, sits down again, plays around with a can of air purifier and looking at the magazines, says: "You haven't read them – now put them all away." I tell him that he is taking me for himself. He puts all the magazines away, one by one. He lies down again.

Then he approaches me, trying to scratch my hands with his nails, and to kick me. I have to contain him – to be very energetic with him. This is not the first time, and his physical attacks towards me have become more frequent. Today he said, "You are a dictator, a tyrant, wanting to rule the whole world. Do you think the world is made of ants? Dictator,

dictator!" I say that he makes me feel a tyrant, and he a victim, and he doesn't see that the tyrant part is his also and it suffocates him.

He continues in his aggression and now takes up the mattress (as before) and arranges it like a shield while he advances towards me, while I have to defend myself. He ends completely rolled up inside the mattress, with me outside.

End of session.

Meltzer's comment: Externalized again, but dramatized, showing the beginning of his ability to oppose the gorilla dictator, which he represents as you but does not experience you to be, in fact. An improvement in his capacity to communicate and not act in the transference.

Session of November 28th, 1979

Mário is lying down and talking about five or six named schoolmates, who graduated in 1974, meanwhile switching the ventilator on and off. I say that perhaps this is his way of telling me what he did in school, with his classmates. He continues, finishes a list of names, turns on the ventilator, then turns it off to recite another list of names. It is impossible to talk to him when he is reciting names. There is no way of getting through to him. At every switch of the ventilator it seems that he is punctuating with a full stop, and that he then turns towards me for my reaction.

Meltzer's comment: Like the air purifier, this is a reference to your talking and his fear of succeeding in silencing you. A new type of game that you must resist – it is his jealousy of your other patients (an endless list) and your home children as well.

Session of November 29th, 1979

Mário says "Good afternoon" and holds out his hand; "here we are again for our afternoon routine"; and he begins to talk, following the same programme as before.

Meltzer's comment: Worried about being able to silence you.

I tell him that today he is different from yesterday, that he is more agitated, as shown by swinging his arms with the cushion. "The only thing that's the same is what you are saying." He sings a number of romantic songs. And he continues the radio-programme. He is the speaker and the listener. He represents two people of a relationship.

Meltzer's comment: These songs are what he fears your other patients sing and that you prefer them to him.

Session of December 17th, 1979

This was the first session after Mário had been away on a two-week camp with the school. He begins by singing various songs. I say: "Mário, you sing such sweet songs to me, and you are happy to be back again as I can see by the way talk about yourself. You talk about your feelings, but your feelings are hidden in the song." He doesn't even seem to catch on to what I am saying. He continues singing songs.

Meltzer's comment: His holiday is felt to have kept you waiting, but accompanied by your other patients. He is gratified by the one, and upset by the other.

I say that he is getting ready to go away because at the end of the week the holidays begin, and he wants me to keep everything about him here with me. He continues to sing songs.

Meltzer's comment: Yes. His jealousy of your home-children is strengthened by the holiday approach.

Note: It seems to me that the contact he proposes comes through the material he offers, but there is still a question of whether it is at the same time a defence against pain, so is also an impediment.

Session of December 18th, 1979

The whole session is taken up with itineraries of streets and highways. I tell him that he made his way here, and he is here now, yet he thinks that he is on the way but hasn't arrived yet and hasn't met me. I ask him also to draw the road – it's a geographical representation of him saying what he has felt, what he has experienced on the way. But he doesn't draw it. He continues with a description of the road and, when it is time for him to go he says "See you later" and gives me a kick on the shins.

Meltzer's comment: Your holiday and his fear of you being lost and not returning.

CHAPTER THREE

Technical problems of the analysis

I n this chapter, we can see the deeper focus on some of the technical problems of this analysis, discussed with Dr Meltzer, as these became especially apparent during the next semester of the analysis, from January 1980 onwards.

Session of January 29th, 1980

Mário enters and immediately starts shouting at me:

Mário: Shut up! Otherwise I'll cut your mouth or I'll tie your mouth or I'll cut your hand! What would you rather have done to you?

And he carries on with the business of filling up a page with numbers in decreasing order, then shows me the CIAM student list (his special school). I ask him if he is still going to study at CIAM this year (a decision to be made before he goes on holiday). He nods and tells me to shut up.

Analyst: You feel I am a threat every time I say something. What do you expect me to do? Am I supposed only to listen to you?

Mário: Right.

Analyst: Like a bucket? I just take in everything you say?

Mário: Right. If you don't shut your mouth within ten minutes, I'll cut out your tongue.

I keep on talking, he reaches for me and asks me to show my tongue, so that he can cut it off, and I say that he must be kidding. He grabs the plug from the sink and brings it close to my mouth, then pretends I have swallowed it. This action is repeated a few times. He then threatens:

Mário: I'll destroy everything; I'm going to take everything out of its place and put it all back again.

Analyst: But this isn't real destroying, it's just make-believe destroying – I've never seen you destroy anything in this room.

Now irritated, he lifts up the mattress, switches on the light, hands me a box, opens some cupboards, fills the sink up to the brim and immediately empties it, opens the rest of the cupboards, and then pushes the bench along the floor. Next, he climbs onto the table, looks at me from above, and slides to the couch, without letting his feet touch the floor, where he remains, lying down.

Note: Mário is trying to fulfil his phantasies by facing what "make-believe" is, what "really do it" is, and what "imagining-accomplishing" is. He then returns to his mental state of omnipotent control and total power, as if insulating the experience in order to maintain control over his defence. He divides me in several parts: my talking mouth and tongue, in this instance, the equivalent of a penis inside a vagina; talking is intercourse, producing the babies-words that he rejects as rivals. What he proposes is to eliminate one of the parts to inhibit the production of the words-babies-rivals, without success.

The room is now the interior that he is going to "destroy", with me as an ally (he gives the box-baby-Mário to the hands-mother-Marisa to be looked after). In this way he goes back to the idealization of the baby-mother that allows him to attack the part of the analyst-mother that is having intercourse with the rival father, making other babies (the "talking" analyst). His refusal to listen to me is due to my being part of this phantasy, probably activated by the prolonged separation of the holidays, when he felt excluded and deprived of my care.

Meltzer's comments: 1. It seems pretty clear that Mário has difficulty taking in what you have to say to him, but this may be only a matter of acknowledging the process. I would suggest that an alteration of technique would be in order, for you to insist that you must have a right to think and speak about your own observations and experience with him, but that he is not obliged to listen if he does not wish to do so. In order to implement this it is necessary to think aloud to yourself, in a tone of rumination and pondering, out into the room and not directly to him.

2. Here you have a clear indication that his activity is play and communication which you can interpret, for it indicates that the mouth and anus are not very clearly distinguished in his mind; both being sphincters. But this would apply to the nipple as well; when it goes into the baby's mouth is it for the purpose of feeding or just to stop up the crying mouth because the mother cannot bear the noise; he understands that some process of "taking out" and "putting back" is involved in the mother's services to the baby but is not clear whether this is constructive or destructive; does she take out bad things and put back good ones, or vice versa, or does she just put back the same things she takes out? For instance, what are your interpretations?

3. Now he makes the problem even clearer: that he cannot distinguish between a process which is the opposite and a process which reverses. Clearly, the sliding down indicates the up-at-the-breast and down-at-the-bottom orientations of the problem. You might say that he has not put together these two simultaneous aspects of experience, moving up and down from breast to lap (toilet) and the process of putting out and taking in from his body and mind.

Session of February 14th, 1980

Owing to the Carnival holidays, the next session was to be nearly a week after this one, on Ash Wednesday (February 20th).

Mário comes in, greets me, waits for me to sit whilst he remains standing in the centre of the room, picks up the pillow (which he then holds onto continuously), and begins to recite:[i]

Mário: Bom Retiro, Casa Verde, Carandiru,
Pompéia e Água Branca,
Pompéia e Água Branca,
Zona Leste, Jardim Europa, Centro,
Barra Funda, Santa Cecília, Centro,
Perdizes, Limão,
Perdizes, Limão,

and so on. He did the same in yesterday's session – describing a railway route, with its ramification and deviations.

I tell him that in "playing" in this manner he is trying to alleviate his anxiety about losing himself, feeling lost, not knowing how to get close to me. He tells me to shut my mouth. He continues naming the railway stations:

Mário: Carandiru, Pari, Bela Vista,
Canindé, Parque São Jorge,
Canindé, Parque São Jorge.

I point out that he names the stations in sets of two or three – Daddy, Mummy and Mário. He tells me to shut my mouth and continues. I say he needs to show off that he knows everything, knows all the routes, and that I'm in the place of a frightened baby.

Mário shouts and tries to hit me. I hold him and he kicks the benches. Then he pulls out magazines from the cupboard, throwing them one by one onto the table. He keeps hold of the fourth magazine and sits turning its pages. When he finishes, he lies down, turns off the fan and begins to recite "Summer Nights".

Mário: It is midnight, it is one past midnight, it is two past midnight, it is 3 past midnight, etc… it is 2.42…

Analyst: It's night! What happens to Mário at night? Doesn't he sleep? Does he have nightmares?"

i These are the names of neighbourhoods in the city of São Paulo (translator's note).

Mário throws the cushion at my face to silence me – and continues to tell the time, minute by minute, until he reaches dawn.

End of session.

At this point Dr Meltzer wrote to me with an explanation of his own supervision technique in this case.

Meltzer's comment: I am going to continue to return the material to you with notes which means that (in the spirit of Bion's "abandonment of memory and desire"), I will be reacting to each new piece of material as a new experience. But of course, you cannot do that, as the events of previous sessions will keep coming into your mind. So there will be no direct continuity in my comments, and you must decide from experience of subsequent sessions whether my comments have turned out to be of any use.

February 14th – His demeanour towards you is one of instructor, you being assumed to be ignorant of orientation to the world and particularly that everything is either in two or three groupings (mother–baby, mother–father, baby–father or mother–father–baby,) but the two-group is generally repeated. Only time is linear, but place and person are in groupings. The impression being that time exists only for the third who is left out when two are together. The general theme is a denial of ignorance and assertion of omnipotent control through naming – what Bion calls "binding the constant conjunctions". This is not only non-symbolic (meaningless, using only signs, not symbols) but is anti-symbolic and anti-meaning. You and the fan, as representatives of meaning, must be annihilated. It would be of interest to know if the sequences of place names are in fact sequential in relation to any particular route. The relevance to the missed sessions of the week is not clear.

Session of February 20th, 1980

Mário shakes my hand, but hits it. Standing up, he begins: "Loris, Vitor, Florinda – pre-harvest." I say, "A list of students – is this a game? Well, let's go!" I take a sheet of paper and jot down what he says.

Mário: Monica, Isabel, Roberto Luiz and Luiz – pre-primary.

Eight pre-secondary: Carlos, Claudio, Sergio-Luiz, Marcos Azevedo, Elizabeth, Beatriz and Silvio.

Fifteen – secondary: Rita, Omar, Jogrsé Raul, Fernanda.

Twenty – tertiary: Loris, Paulo, Dirceu and Hermann.

Twenty-four – quarternary: Calegari, Karen, Felix, Claudio.

Twenty-eight: Iece Angel, Bueno, Edson, Milton and Roque.

Thirty-three – room 2: Calegari, Karen, Claudio and Felix.

Room 10: Milton, Florinda, Vitor and Loris.

Room 11: Loris, Paulo, Dirceu and Hermann.

Rooms 14 & 15: Angel, Bueno, Edson, Milton and Roque … (*and so on*).

Note: Mário is very content, beaming, when he sees that I am avidly attentive, and that I can even recite the names of the students with him, which he continues to repeat. I am trying to investigate things that are inaccessible, by means of playful contact, through play-acting in which he is the director of the school and I am his secretary. The satisfaction he gets from my acting is very evident. He sees me as a collaborator, someone he need not oppose, even conversing openly with me, explaining this and that about his school life.

After the session, I wonder if this exploratory conduct could be useful in increasing my contact with him.

Meltzer's comment: He has now moved from the preoccupation with the outside world and the overwhelming problem of orientation in time and space *vis-à-vis* the two plus three minus body relationship and the problem of loneliness and its acute awareness of time. The central theme is now inside – the school, inside the mother = you, with your mind full of children (patients and home-children).

Again his approach is to bind with names and to organize in groups and categories. But there is also an indication that time exists in this world as well, but it is only signalled by a bell and its frame of reference is mysterious, perhaps arbitrary. I assume that you have recorded these sessions and that the list of names and sequences is accurate. It is noticeable that the sequence – say of pre-secondary – is reversed, while others are obviously rearranged. This must mean that he is reading from a visual memory, sometimes from right to left, sometimes left to right, other times in a more random way. Certain hints of meaning begin to enter, as if by accident ("careful how you cross the road"). The groupings are apparently random as to sex as with any other indicator, which may imply sexual innocence. The school bus leaving would have also the significance of birth. The overall impression, despite the introduction of school (study, learning, exams, etc), is one of boredom and waiting for graduation day and the bus leaving. The sense that he is the director comes, I think, from the powerful feeling of control based on naming and categorizing, very characteristic of the latency period, when knowing the name is felt to contain implicitly all possible knowledge of the object named ("electricity" or "carburettor", for instance).

Session of February 21st, 1980

When I go to call Mário, I find him locked in the toilet, knocking on the door to get out, as he could not turn the doorknob. This had happened several times before. I therefore proceed to free him.

He greets me and continues to recite the CIAM list of students from 1975. I express my willingness to continue, as in the previous session.

I am struck by just how this boy is capable of using his memory as an archive, describing the time, place and circumstances relating to an event that stimulated some emotion in him, and to which he appears to have no access. Therefore, playing theatrical roles or describing events are his means of expressing what is going on in his mind.

He continues the same cataloguing of CIAM students, the groups and the graduation. Then twenty minutes into the session he abruptly leaves, closing the door behind him (normally, he asks permission to leave, but not today). I get the impression he was headed for the toilet as he appears to need to urinate urgently. When he is finished, he is unable to open the door to the room. He bangs on the door, and I tell him to push it harder, as it isn't locked. He eventually manages to open the door.

I say: "You are finding obstacles in the path between us, and one of us is captive – either you or me. The baby is locked in! The wicked director has imprisoned baby Mário."

End of session.

Meltzer's comment: Now the issue of being able to leave the school of mother's inside emerges in action, and the claustrophobic meaning of this place becomes apparent, first coming *out* of the toilet and later coming *into* your room. This may indicate that the denial of meaning is not only to deny confession, but also persecuting (claustrophobic) anxiety (locked in the toilet) and depressive pain (unable to get back to you).

Session of February 22nd, 1980

Mário continues to play the director.

I make it quite clear that he, as the director, is suffocating baby Mário, who is greatly in need of feeding and growing-up like Marisa, and that the director places himself in between and prevents it. I tell him that the director talks and talks about unimportant things, whilst the poor little baby is starving, left forgotten and unattended. I say that the director is being wicked.

Mário carries on looking at me, smiling, allowing me to interrupt.

Analyst: That's it, poor boy! Here's baby-Mário and here's mother-Marisa, but the wicked director locks the baby up.

It seems to me that he continues to be very pleased with my interventions, but carries on in his role of director.

Analyst: How useless this director is. He never shuts up! His days are numbered.

Whilst I was talking, he was trying to hit me with a cushion. Then he stops playing the part of the director and lies down.

Mário: Let's see what baby you're talking about!

Analyst: It's you! When you are scared and needing to take in the "food" that I have to offer you, you come along with this gorilla-director stuff that suffocates the baby.

Mário: What baby are you talking about? It's a paranoid baby. It shouldn't be here! It should be left to get cold, and hungry, and with no one to look after it. Your days are numbered! You have six days in which to end this argument. I'm not going to let you win. I'll kill you.

(He looks satisfied.)

Analyst: You, gorilla, will kill baby-me?

Mário: (*shouting*) This baby is paranoid! There – at school – it's been there a long time. It's this size! (He holds his thumb and forefinger apart.) It's seventeen years old! When it was four, I took it to the school's director, and I locked it in the imagination of a secretary-lady. And there it will remain! And it will never, never grow up! You are paranoid! Wanting the baby back! It has to stay there whilst I'm not alive! (*parapraxis*)

Analyst: That's right! Because you are not really able to live without the baby-you, which needs to be cared for by both of us. But the gorilla-director doesn't let it.

Mário: No! Only if you win. Otherwise only when I'm dead!

Meltzer's comment: The introduction of a personification of the persecutory anxiety ("director") is your way of giving a name to the anxiety and may not correspond to the structure of his personality; at least there is not clear evidence for such a structure as yet. But the "baby" does emerge in the previous session and can be talked about concretely. What does emerge is a differentiation between the dependent (locked-in, locked-out) baby and the know-it-all latency child with his naming and categorizing. The attempt to silence you with the cushion also suggests an infantile anxiety, of being smothered by the breast. The challenge he issues is a kind of treasure hunt in which, as in many fairy tales, the hero has to find something in a limited period of time or forfeit his life, in the case of heroes, or the baby, as with heroines (say in "Rumplestiltskin"). You are a heroine who must *find* your baby before it dies of cold and starvation. Clearly you must find it inside yourself ("school") where it has been growing as an embryo and must risk your life, as every woman does in childbirth. He has picked up your naming of "director" and "secretary-lady"[ii] to indicate his state of earlier confusion about his masculine and feminine tendencies and about the sexual relation between the parents in producing the baby. Now it *is* suggested that some aspect of him may die if you do not succeed in locating this "paranoid" baby, i.e. that the urgency is not only yours, but his as well.

Session of March 17th, 1980

Mário enters, greets me, and starts to talk about a football championship in which the results of the games are always, for example, 4-3 or 2-1. To get his attention, I comment in a loud voice that Mário is giving me so much news, talking so much about the championship, that all I can do is listen; but I will take notes of all this information. As I speak I make for the box and open it to take out a pen and sheet of paper.

For the first time he intervenes and prevents me from rummaging in the box. I tell him that this is the role he has given me himself and so I must perform it (I am acting). But he is vehement: "Be quiet and don't talk! Absolutely quiet! If not I will kick you!"

The situation escalates and he attacks me, threatening me in order that I remain quiet, that I do not "get into the box".

Mário: You will never see the contents of this box.

Analyst: Your fear is that I'll show you the contents of what you have hidden in the box, and you do everything to prevent us from coming together, for example, by telling stories and more stories.

Mário: Shut your mouth!

ii The patient had named himself director, and me, secretary.

When the session is over Mário takes his leave shaking hands like old friends who have been acting together in a play.

Meltzer's comment: The "championship" is being enacted in the playroom and seems to have the meaning of who is the "father" (feeder) and who is the "listener" (fed) – a reversal of baby-breast. In that case, the "miracle of the boy" = the miracle of the breast, the secret of the breast's creativity. While this could be taken at either anal or genital level, the latter two areas would not encompass the mystery-of-the-mother's-body which appears to be central. The threats to "kick", transforming the breast into the football, transform the "championship" into a more whole-object competition, baby versus mother, rather than the part-object mouth versus nipple. This latter level seems to me to be more essential for his role as guardian of the box and its mysteries, makes his tongue related to his mind as the nipple is the guardian of the breast. A more cogent and evolutive level.

It is heartening that he does not so much object to your taking notes of what he says. This probably would please him, play in with his phantasy, and does not seem to be a useful procedure. It is the "rummaging" in the box to which he takes exception, i.e. searching out the heart of his mystery.

Session of March 18th, 1980

Mário: Today, championship, division B, games… (*and so on*).

  Analyst: Ah! Let's take down the important announcements that Mário is going to make.

  I take the box, open it and take out a sheet of paper and a pen.

  Mário (*replacing the things in the box*): No way! Shut it! Don't touch anything in there! If you don't remain absolutely quiet, in your place, you'll get it from me!

  Analyst: I can't be absolutely quiet in my place watching you attack the poor Mário-baby.

  He tries to hit me, to control me so that I stay still.

  Analyst: But why so many stories?

Mário: It's necessary – to get into your little head and leave you confused!

Analyst: You are seriously committed to ensuring that I do not discover the contents of this box.

Mário: You are not going to see, never again, and you'll never know.

Analyst: I know that the baby is hidden in there.

(The session is of quite a dramatic nature and I am encouraging him to make contact with me, whilst he also permits some contact.) There is a moment when he lies down and asks to rest, and for me to be quiet: dumb, blind, and still.

Analyst: Can't I even breathe?

Mário: You're allowed to breathe.

He turns off the fan and says that it will only be turned on again when he leaves.

When leaving, he says: "Stay there with your fan."

Meltzer's comment: "Get into your little head and leave you confused" – precisely the object of the reversal. But your opposition and his control gradually exhaust his reversal and he collapses into passivity, allow you to breathe (talk) and to be left alone at the end with your fan (the talking-coitus with the fan penis that takes away all the bad talk he has put into head to make you into the confused baby-breast).

Session of March 20th, 1980

This session is the last of the week. Mário comes in and, as usual, begins talking about the championship, the football divisions and their teams, but eyeing me the whole time. Ever since the previous session he has kept saying that I have to remain quiet; that I'm an idiot, a donkey, stupid and incompetent. He says that I will never achieve anything and that all psychoanalysis is pretentious.

His behaviour in the room is that everything in it is his, and that nothing belongs to me, not even an opportunity or a break in which to speak; the fan is turned off and on as and when it suits him, for he is the owner and I, his slave. If I talk, he threatens me in all sorts of ways: "I'll make you stop breathing, got it?" or (walking over to the cupboard in the room), "I'll use everything in here to attack you!"

Note: It appears to me that this situation is now being lived by him consciously – this is the young gorilla, the bearer of triumph and arrogance. The other aspect is phobic – that is, the fear of relating to the other. There is the baby, in need, yet prevented from being cared for, not allowed to come out of hiding. There is a self-sufficient child, a child-adult who is his own father and mother, born of the fear of giving himself into the care of his real father and mother.

Meltzer's comment: This outpouring, in no way intended to enlighten or enrich you as the baby, is to be taken as what Bion calls the "super"-ego – a figure based on projective identification with a part-object that merely proclaims its superiority. Iit is similar to Mrs Klein's "breast that feeds itself"; its intention is to project feelings of smallness, weakness, poverty, ignorance and envy. If you, as the breast, resist this reversal, you become the football-breast that will be "kicked" – "take away your breathing".

Session of March 25th, 1980

Mário has a bandage on a finger of his left hand.
  Analyst: What happened?
  He doesn't reply.
  Analyst: You think that I know what happened.
  Mário: CIAM students – Luiz, Artur… (*and so on*).
  I listen to him for a few minutes; from time to time, he looks at me.
  Analyst: I say to you: "How nice – see how he knows everything, see he is a teacher, see he is a director, see much he knows. See, he knows how to control everything! See, what a genius! And me? A stupid thing, a donkey, an ignorant mule – incompetent!" (I am using his words from recent sessions.)

But he does not stop talking and I have to speak above him in order to get a word in during his pauses.

Analyst: Look, what a lot of things – how wonderful! But what use are they to you? I think it looks like Mário-father talking with Marisa-mother about a paranoid baby.

Mário: This paranoid baby ought to be locked up in school and never allowed to go out.

Analyst: He is a sadistic father! And what about his mother?

Mário: His mother died. But it's impossible to free the baby that is suffering from hunger and nearly dying; if it were freed, its mother could make it into a great man! But this will never happen, only if I'm conquered! Ha-ha-ha-ha-ha-ha! Ha-ha-ha-ha-ha-ha! (*The baby gorilla laugh.*)

Meltzer's comment: The reversal having collapsed and the possibility of feeding the Mário-baby having now appeared, the persecutor of the mother-baby relationship intrudes between mother and wounded baby (cut finger) and it is necessary to do a kind of combat with this persecutor to feed the baby, for otherwise it feels that its mother is dead (silent) and cannot nurture it "into a great man". This persecutor may represent a bad father but I doubt it, at this point, as it seems to claim no relationship to you as breast-mother; it only claims the power to interfere.

Session of April 22nd, 1980

There was no session the previous day, a Monday, due to a national holiday.

Mário talks about the championship. The results are always 2-1 or 3-2. He pauses.

I tell him that he talks and talks in order to ride over us - so that we think about nothing except what he is saying. He orders me to shut my mouth.

He finishes talking about the championship and asks me if there will be a session next Friday (referring to the absence of a session the day before).

Analyst: I don't know. If I have a free slot, I'll see you. Would you like that?

He is much calmer and more receptive. He lies down.

Mário (*kicking me*): You pack-mule! Incompetent!

Analyst: What pack? Yours? The one you don't want and that you give to me to carry?

Mário: Ha! Ha!

(This interests him. He is more ready for contact, and is much more present with me in the room.)

Analyst: And what do we make of the fact you call me a donkey, an incompetent, yet as me for a session next Friday?

He makes loud noises and gestures to frighten me, accompanied by movements to scare me away. Then, lying down, he occupies the final twenty minutes by watching the clock, counting with his finger and reciting the time in a low voice.

Mário: 1.05, 1.10. 1.15, 1.20, 1.25, 1.30. The whole world and you, 1.35, 1.40, 1.45… The world is news, 1.50…

Meltzer's comment: The reversal again until he can ask for the lost session to be replaced. But he feels also that you are triumphant at his need, and returns to being abusive, not in the reversal, but lying down as the resentful baby, watching the time, precious, counting it to be sure it isn't stolen from him. "The whole world" = the breast "and you" = the whole-object mother.

Session of April 28th, 1980

Mário arrives late (it is a Monday) and immediately asks "Am I late?" followed by another question: whether there will be a session on Friday (the Thursday being a national holiday).

Analyst: There will be no replacement unless a slot opens up. I am now noting your interest and need.

His eyes are filled with tears and I ask if he is going to cry. He says he has a cold. Meanwhile, his lips are quivering and mucus drips from his nose. I tell him that there are tissues in the toilet if he would like to blow his nose. He goes and wipes his nose before returning.

The session continues with him reciting the results of old football games. I say that Mário is with Marisa, recounting anything that makes him feel big as he is frightened of feeling small, very, very small, and he needs Marisa to help him grow. He raises no objections and watches me attentively, with deep interest.

The session continues with another story.

He occupies the final 10 to 15 minutes by lying down and following the hands of the clock, talking the whole time and constantly touching the clock's glass face.

I tell him that he is messing around, that he is entertaining himself with his body – with his ideas, and all this gives him the same sort of pleasure as would, for example, playing with his penis.

He tells me to shut up; he says I'm a fool, a donkey, an incompetent, etc.

Meltzer's comment: Here you see the infantile possessiveness and the reversal operating simultaneously and finally the reversal conquers, temporarily but without triumph or contempt, only for relief, and then gives way to the baby count-down. Here I think you are wrong in your interpretation and deserve his scolding.

Some technical questions sent to Dr Meltzer

1) For well over a month, in both the first and last of the weekly sessions, Mário has talked of the results of games played the previous Sunday, for example: "Palmeiras beat Corinthians 4-3. São Paulo beat Santos 4-3." (These are football teams from São Paulo in the First National Division and he spends a considerable part of the sessions proclaiming the results, but always with the same score: 4-3.) I speak to him about the matches that he keeps imagining when he is not with me, and of the fact that the score is always 4-3. I ask him what the 4 is – is it mother, father,

Mário and Marcelo (his brother)? And 3, is it mother, father and Mário? I carry on, suggesting all the possible combinations, and purposely include the 4 to 3 that he constantly uses. He tries to physically attack me whilst I am speaking. In other sessions, he has changed the results of the games to 2-1.

At this point I am considering this material from two angles: firstly that of form – what functioning capacity does his psychic apparatus have and what is it doing; how does his learning arise from experience, etc., and if we need to resort to Bion. Secondly, that of content: the meanings, anxieties, and the relationship between his psychic content and the psychic structure he has to hold it.

Meltzer's comment: The nature of this infantile transference of intense and greedy dependence on the breast (your mind) and nipple (the clock) and the father's penis (the fan) brings severe separation anxiety and leaves him vulnerable to a persecutor who ridicules him and disparages you. He tends to defend against this by reversal through projective identification, making you into the ridiculed, dependent baby whose greed must be savagely controlled so that it does not rip out the nipple (the contents of the box) and take control of the breast and time and the whole world and you.

I would think that this material is adequately understood in Mrs Klein's terms and the "resolution of the depressive position" as outlined in *The Psychoanalytical Process*. Bion's concepts regarding male and female content symbols in thought disorders do not seem to present themselves. He presents, structurally, a problem of inadequate splitting-and-idealization, or he cannot yet form the combination of an idealized part of the self with an idealized object as a foundation of security.

2) Mário recounts stories, some of which are from very young children's literature, such as "The Three Little Pigs" and *Sítio do Pica-Pau Amarelo* (a popular series of books for children written by Monteiro Lobato), albeit with some changes. Thus, he might use a story's structure but change the names of the

characters. The story of the three little pigs, for example, became that of three little boys, André, Mário, and Rubin, whilst the wolf became a bad lion, and the moral of the story was that first you do the chores and then have fun. As for *Sítio do Pica-Pau Amarelo*, he has three characters – Silvio, Mário and Horatio, with Horatio being a happy-go-lucky sort who says: "The other two are an extinct species", and "They don't make them like they used to." He names characters after himself in his stories and reuses names for characters in several stories. As he tells a story, a character will be unmasked and revealed as a copy of an original that is not actually in the story. This recourse that he has come up with allows the character to free himself from a threat that, it seems to me, becomes very real as the story progresses.

I believe it is worth looking at part of a story that he began to tell, on and off, about a year ago – "A Santa do Pau Oco" (an episode from the *Sítio do Pica-Pau Amarelo* television series). His story-telling recalled the *telenovelas* on television, in which the title or even a trailer of a forthcoming series would be shown before it was scheduled to come on air. However, Mário's "episodes" follow a time-interval different to that used by the *telenovelas*. Whilst recounting his stories there are moments when he becomes so emotionally involved that I wonder whether he might be hallucinating, actually "seeing" the characters. I got the impression he was making "mental toys" and then releasing them into the room to play with them.

Meltzer's comment: His stories functions as do dreams in adult analysis, or children's play, as a continuous narrative that describes the ebb and flow of narcissistic organization of parts of the personality and object relations. It is this ebb and flow that needs to be followed and rendered as interpretations of *organizational* progress in the analysis, demonstrating how the narcissism aggravates the anxieties it seeks to defend against, while the object relationships relieve these persecutions but bring him in touch with depressive feelings, especially in connection with the separations, changes in time arrangements, moments when you fail to understand, etc.

3) The physical aggression occurs every time I speak to him, interrupting the story; and, occasionally, when I stay listening to him until the end of the story. There is almost always a period when he lies down and is quiet. On many occasions I have used this time to talk to him, as it is generally the time that he listens to me, allows contact and answers me. I could say that these moments result from a sequence established by Mário, and that they allow me to describe what I observe from his behaviour with me, taking into account the sequence and the distance he maintains between us. The typical sequence is: initial contact at the start of the session; then the performance of a story (distance); followed by the end of the performance (potential contact); then he lies down, enumerating lists and numbers, or telling the time until the end of the session (distance); and ends by calling me names – "stupid", "donkey", "incompetent", threatening to kick me or displaying other means of aggression if don't keep quiet (contact). (By "contact", I mean with the external-analyst object.)

Meltzer's comment: Where this sort of acting-in-the-transference has replaced play-as-communication, it is probably necessary, in order to be listened to and not "jammed", to "think-aloud" rather then "interpret to" the patient. The sequence in the session corresponds, as I have suggested, to certain defences giving way to the infantile crying and contact, but as the end approaches there is the tendency again to turn against you, especially if he feels you do not understand the intensity of his anxieties about the approaching separation.

4) Other details observed in his conduct over the past months include his holding the sofa-cushion throughout almost the whole the session. It is an integral part of his body during his performances, given on foot in the centre of the room, and which are always enacted with much drama and bodily expression. I remember that, at the outset of the analysis, he waved his arms in the air and moved like a puppet. When he is seated on the sofa, he usually plays around with the cushion, cuddling it, opening his mouth and lightly squeezing and stretching it, only letting it

go in order to lie down after positioning the cushion as a pillow for his head. Should I consider it in terms of an accompanying object, or a transitional object?

Meltzer's comment: This behaviour regarding the cushion is surely breast-related – the possessiveness, the tendency to abuse, the sensuality, the clinging dependence, the fusion and separateness. It contrasts with the disarticulated, puppet behaviour when, at the start, he had no focus – what Bion calls "O" and Money-Kyrle ("Cognitive Development" in the *Collected Papers*) calls the "home" around which the body-ego forms itself and its concept-building. It is not a "transitional object" but a "representation" in the transference of your breast-mind, but could easily become a transitional object if the sado-masochistic and fetishistic trend were to take hold.

Sessions of July to August, 1980

I shall continue now with the transcription of some sessions from July and August, 1980.

Session of July 31st, 1980

In this session Mário is both the train and the conductor, boarding people onto the train, shouting out the names of the stations and imitating the chug-chug-chug noises of the engine. It stops at every station with some passengers getting off and others getting on, and so on up to the end of the session. At every station he says: "Those wishing to get off – please do so; those wishing to come aboard – please do so; to those leaving us – we wish you a good day's work; to those joining us – we hope you'll feel comfortable and enjoy your trip!" And then he does the chug-chug noise until the next station, and so on, with each stop being named after a real train station.

I tell him that he is talking about the exchanges between us; the passengers that get on and off are the things I tell him and that go inside him, and things that come out of him and get inside me, and so forth. As I talk he continues his act, imitating the train, etc.

Session of August 1st, 1980

In this session he carries on exactly as he did in the last session, monotonously repeating the same sequence of events. I tell him that he is talking about the programmed farewells and encounters that he uses to keep control of what arises inside him at the times when we meet or part. When I say this he carries on with his act, but in silence, moving around the room, and at that moment it seemed to me this was his answer to my interpretation. Then he resumed his full act, with the announcements and everything.

This situation makes me feel powerless to break into the vicious circle he is in. I tell him so and add that he is afraid of being invaded by what I say, of feeling impotent, and that by acting in this way, he ends up with everything: the space and the attention, trying to trap my mind and cling onto it, in the same way as with the cushion.

Note: The train, the station, getting in and out, all evoke symbolic elements – the train progressing is his genitals, the Mário-train getting to the Marisa-station; the train running on the rails is a safe route. This acting makes him feel protected from the anguish of not knowing the way. In every session there is a route that results from the emotional situation being developed with me – and the defence is to be the train that simply follows its predetermined course, both out and back. He is forced to cover his route! His fear is to have a destination from which he cannot escape, and that is my counter-transference. The sequence he follows within a session and the sequence from one session to the next seems to be the "mother" that Mário has constructed.

Meltzer's comment: The processes of projection and introjection are now in the forefront of the material. While it seems to refer to babies entering and leaving the mother's body, being comfortable inside and enjoying work outside, it must also have some reference to his coming and going from your office on the one hand, and to the food coming in and faeces going out of his own body, on the other hand. But he has not yet been able to narrow the range of these possibilities by introducing the emotionality, so it remains repetitive, lacking in feeling and potentially endless. It must be the therapist's task to select one of the many meanings to focus the attention and bring forth the feelings. This you do, focusing on the problem of separation and reunion, introducing a depressive atmosphere. But he breaks out of it again and thus projects the incipient depressive feelings into you.

But instead of following the separation theme, you have switched over to a more sexual area because you have perhaps mistaken the depressive feeling of hopelessness for a feeling of powerlessness to alter his state of mind. I would think that, although the sexual theme is surely there, it is far less loaded with feelings and much more filled with omnipotence than the theme of infantile dependence and fear of separation. I think you can be fairly confident that of the paired activities, the projective (evacuation) and the introjective (feeding), the separation anxieties are more severe in the latter. So that would need to be approached more slowly, only after having dealt with that aspect in which the train represents his faeces and the problem of being able to retain, control and find a suitable receptacle to receive his debris. You appear to be unduly disturbed by the repetitiveness of his actions and wish the interpretations to have a "mutative" impact. This they will only have by way of mobilizing his affects, as when he carries on but in silence. I would think that he became depressed at that point and that this was a clear indicator that the separation theme should be pursued, with emphasis on his need for his Marisa-rubbish bin.

Discussion

These supervisions were the starting point for trying to apply this approach to Mário's analysis and it seemed to have found fertile soil, for I was finding it almost impossible to analyse him. I was despondent in fact about whether he and I were actually viable as a psychoanalytic pair. Did I have the technical and personal resources to analyse him? Could I endure a prolonged phase of his monotonously repeating lists, denying real contact? But Meltzer's suggestion that I do not talk directly to him but instead maintain an attitude of "rumination and reflection", of saying what I thought, could prove useful. And to follow an interpretative plan using more concrete language in order to address his phantasies.

However, it took me some time to assimilate this knowledge before I could try applying it in a practical way. I even felt it was so difficult to continue his analysis that I questioned my technical qualifications and whether it was actually possible for me to analyse him. Driven by these questions, I tried to evaluate what advances had been made after five semesters of analysis, either in his relationship with me or in his external life. As far as the analytic work went, he regularly attended the four sessions per week and showed that he was "in charge" of his schedule. In fact, his mother told me that he made a point of coming to the session and that arriving on time mattered to him.

He looks more expressive and in touch with the environment; his mouth movements no longer give the impression of his tongue lolling loose in his mouth, and his body posture is also more articulated when compared with the puppet-like disarticulation seen in the beginning. He communicates with me directly on arrival and during the final part of the session, when he verbally rejects me and denies what I tell him. For the past three semesters he has grabbed a cushion as soon as he comes in and holds on to it constantly while standing up and enacting his stories. The content in his stories has become clearer and less confusing.

What seems to me unchanged is his adherence to the dramatized storytelling sequences that he establishes, organizing the time and space of the session in order to talk without being interrupted: that is, his refusal to listen. His parents think that he is "more alive", more "bonded" to them. He has accepted the move from CIAM (the special school where he spent six years) to a regular school; he still isolates himself at family gatherings, staying in a room and enacting his storytelling. These were the improvements.

He masturbates with a certain regularity; he dislikes being questioned regarding his attraction to girls or interest in dating. He is enthusiastic about going to his grandmother's house with his parents, but once there, he shuts himself in a room and begins telling his stories out loud.

Meanwhile, after reading *Explorations in Autism,* it became clear to me that I should delve deeper into Melanie Klein's technique, and, reviewing the situation, I wrote to Dr Meltzer in January 1981 to ask his advice about how to proceed with the analysis. I explained that my impression was always that Mário was only present physically, and his mind was occupied entirely with his storytelling in order to his fear of making proper contact with me, which would awaken unknown feelings in him. He transfers feelings onto the things in the room. But I could not understand why he felt so inadequately equipped to face the emotionality of human contact, or how analysis could help him become so equipped and to learn from experience.

The picture of Mário formed in association with Meltzer's comments was that structurally, Mário had a problem with unsuitable splitting-and-idealization, being unable to form a continuity between an idealized part of himself and an idealized object, forming a safe base. He made use of adhesive identification with a two-dimensional object because he had not developed the notion of internal space. He had become addicted to the use of autistic objects.

I had various doubts which I formulated and sent to Dr Meltzer. These were:

1) The use of reversal indicates that he uses the mechanism of projective identification, so there is a configuration of the three-dimensional object. However, he very easily loses this level of organization, returning to the two-dimensional object level.

Does this mean that he makes no distinction between a good object that is absent, and the presence of a persecutory object?

2) What are autistic objects?

3) Does Mário present obsessive mechanisms derived from autism as autistic defences against object relations?

4) Do you believe Mário presents a residual autistic disturbance?

I felt it was necessary to synthesize this experience theoretically, and in the course of this, I wondered: at what point was Mário's development halted? What were the fears and what the traumatic situation that he repeated so compulsively? What were his defensive resources? Which of his needs needed to be satisfied for his development to proceed?

His first need, shown in his defence, seemed to be to have an environment that could provide a simple, repetitive routine experience of being a baby, around which primary disassociation (splitting-and-idealization of the object and of the self) and the organization of personality can take place. Mário shows inadequate splitting and idealization in which the object is not securely established. The storytelling sequences, as well as the fragmentation of the emotional experiences, seem to have the aim of providing a repetitive and simple alternative. They could result from a need to adhere to the object. The physical fact of adhering to the object, or of having the nipple in the mouth, is replaced by a mental product made of stories that keeps his mind united. This acts as a containing skin enabling him to be separate from his mother when awake without his body-self disintegrating. Bick considered this the pre-requisite for adequate splitting and idealization, and for differentiating good from bad. The story-object to which Mário adheres and that maintains his mental unity, also protects him from abandonment and perhaps from the imminent disaster of falling into an abyss if a space emerges (between him and the other). However, it prevents him from developing because it severely impedes him from having a vital interchange that would nourish him and help him grow up. This live interchange of projection-introjection between him and me only happens on occasion. Most of the time, he is inside his characters, and his entire mind stays inside the story, giving the impression that there is no available part of the mind mind to which I can talk and establish contact.

The clinical material suggests that the nipple represents a dangerous part of his object, like an intruder that interferes with his access to the contents of the breast. Thus the nipple-less breast seems to be a good object, into which he can go and help himself. If the breast insists on having a nipple (a precursor to his fantasies about the penis) the solution is for Mário to become the nipple-penis, seizing control of their attributes and becoming the one that controls and repairs the maternal object, as an exclusive provider. This is what continually happens in the transference. So the experiencing of jealousy and rivalry is deprived of meaning, which meets his demand for exclusive possession of the object. In another configuration, Mário's object seems to be good when it is emptied of the penis as it then becomes passive and enslaved – I must be quiet, passive, without a tongue (penis) so as not to talk (have intercourse); he is the mouth-tongue-penis; when I speak, I threaten to destroy the idealization that his mouth is the source of all pleasure for the breast (maternal object). The behaviour of holding the cushion represents the breast-mind in transference, and there we see the possessiveness, the tendency to abuse sensuality, the dependence on attaching oneself, on adhering and on fusion. This behaviour is opposed to the disarticulated puppet-like behaviour shown in the first year of analysis, when he lacked what Money-Kyrle calls the "home" around which the body-ego forms itself. Intolerance of separation is manifest in the need for physical contact, for constant attention, or for constant verbalization, all in order to keep the parts of the self united.

I would like to say more about his defensive resource of storytelling.

The stories all have a sequence, a guiding thread aimed at cancelling internal and external discontinuities, allowing no space for interruption or the non-scheduled. Instead of an internalized relationship with me, the sequence produces a continuous, uniform, sequential object, one that does not suddenly disappear leaving him abandoned to himself, threatened by death. The emotions that are awoken by contact with me, and the fantasies that emerge from this contact, cannot cross this barrier and expose his psychic life to threat. Of course, this barrier fails, which is when he becomes disturbed and resorts to rebuilding it through figures, codes and lists.

The stories are the verbalization of fantasies that emerge through contact with external reality. There are sessions in which the verbalization is already an action in the sense that the words are already the realization of the fantasy in which to name with a word is already to possess or to have accomplished; that is where the mental activity jumps from fantasy to realization. (Meltzer calls this phenomenon the use of primitive obsessive mechanisms, in addition to the already known defensive use.) In the transference, Mário uses these obsessive mechanisms in an established way, indicating that this is how his personality has been organized, possibly since the infantile autism, and now serves to dominate the growing complexity of his object relations. These obsessive mechanisms, says Meltzer, like the autistic mechanisms, are intended to simplify the experience by separating the experience of the object into sensorial and motor modes. Hence Mário's mentally handicapped, child-like appearance.

Mário has a store of useless knowledge. For instance, he knows the names of all the Gold Cup winners since 1960; all CIAM undergraduate students since 1974; all the match scores from the last four national football championships, etc. He also demonstrates knowledge of history, geography and the Bible, and he seems to read up on these subjects in order to validate his fantasies about his mother's body, to be sure of his power and to demarcate geographic territories in the face of the threat of invasion. This "knowledge" is itself imprisoned in its organization, with separately stored facts, and is intended to be retained and catalogued than used in his developmental process.

The omnipotent processes of invasive possessiveness and control are linked with his symbolic equation of separation from the maternal object and death. This equation is related to his difficulty in introjecting the maternal object, of allowing it to breathe and move. Thus, the objects imprisoned in his organization and separated from each other cannot be used (or united). On the occasions when he realizes he is separated from the maternal object (as in the transference), and is outside it, he feels anxious: the objects are free and they are outside his control. This is, for example, what happens close to longer separations (weekends, school holidays); and these anxieties intensify his omnipotent control and object separation mechanisms, for the danger lies in the fact that undoing this obsessive organization will result in a loss of the boundary that protects him from invasion, liable to fall into an idealized situation of total fusion with the object (autism). But, as previously said, this obsessive organization interferes in the adaptation process because the oversimplification of obsessive thinking impairs the experiencing and emotional response to the complexity of the world. However, the severity of a post-autistic state is related to the degree of disturbance in the organization of the mental space (that is, the differentiation between inside and outside the self, and inside and outside the object). In order for Mário's development to continue it is necessary to once again establish this interchange of projection and introjection, releasing the "locked" emotions in the obsessive organization, so that he can maintain a "feeding relationship" (mouth-nipple-breast) with me.

CHAPTER FOUR

Fighting the use of autistic objects

This chapter covers a period (1981–1982) in which I focussed on the problem of dealing with Mário's use of autistic objects, and made some experimental explorations. From April 1981, I decided to make my presence more emphatic in order to tackle this problem. It seemed it was not enough to simply speak aloud, to ponder, to show that I am present; this approach still tolerated the use of autistic objects. So from this time, when he came in and started telling his stories or enumerating his lists, I tried standing up myself, in a more confrontational way.

When I saw, for example, that he was listing a numerical sequence with an interval of four figures, I spoke the next number in the sequence, showing him that I had solved the riddle. He became furious, hitting me and trying to wrestle back control by forcing me to go back to "my place". On other occasions he would threaten me, assaulting me with the cushion, the footstool, the box, kicking out and climbing onto the table so that he felt more powerful than me.

I began to feel there was real contact. He seemed to be responsive when forced to interrupt his autistic style relationship. His emotions were more "controlled" and it seemed to me that it was worthwhile carrying on with the new approach, which allowed me to compete with the defensive sequence of stories – his autistic object.

However, I felt this active fight against the autistic objects seemed to be non-analytic and rather pedagogic. To analyse this situation is to show him that he is attached to the autistic object for fear of real contact with emotions that he can bear no longer, fear of what he actually does during the sessions, as seen from his material. It is as if I am passing on my feelings of impotence about the possibility of analysing a mind under these conditions, and my intolerance of waiting for psychic changes that do not take place.

After these reflections, my attempts to interrupt him became constant, a struggle against his use of autistic objects. I question him and ask for explanations, guessing the next number in a sequence, pointing out that he uses historical data any way that pleases him. I took the risk of trying to prevent him from using up the entire session with his lists, to get him to understand he must allow me some space. We had to try this, and he needed to look for other resources. He did respond by limiting the use of his autistic object during the sessions.

Frances Tustin believes that the autistic object must be fought. But, if I believe that my role is to analyse him, my approach should not be based on fighting: rather, I must show him that he does not want to be interrupted by me; that he wants to stay united with his autistic object and to have no contact with me. I must demonstrate to him that he is not against analysis, that he is not, in fact, against anything because he is not connected to anybody; he is with "his objects" instead of really being in touch with me, and this makes him feel composed, without suffering anxiety.

His parents know that his development is retarded; they want to help him and bring him to analysis. But, what about Mário himself? What role does he attribute to me? I listen to him, I see him everyday and I talk with him. He feels that he has a place where he is listened to, looked at, his performances appreciated.

In the game of projective identifications he is a mother who has a lot of knowledge, who is busy and cannot pay attention to a baby (the analyst) who should in turn be still and quiet in order to neither disturb nor interrupt the mother (himself). But, at the same time, he has a real experience of being heard and interrupted (the analyst as a different mother), as a baby that can speak and make space for a mother who is fully available for him.

In one session (August 17th, 1981), Mário talked about a very large country with a variety of regions, some very hot and populated, others very cold with Eskimos and igloos near the Pole, and other very fertile ones. He said, "The Amazon region can be explored, but carefully, and it has a lot of wealth. The other region cannot be explored because it has a lot of Indians and is very hot. The savannah regions – nothing, they are barren." He addressed me directly throughout this metaphorical story, looking at me all the time in high spirits, as if there were hopes for his own explorations. My notes from 1981 are witness to my struggle against the autistic objects, such that at one point, for a period, I experimented with having the mother participating in the analytic process.

Experimental explorations

By "experimental explorations" I mean initiatives taken by the analyst that do not conform to the usual analytical process and may not be suited to all cases, even those that present similar difficulties. Thus, at the end of November, 1981, Mário's mother began participating in one of the sessions each week.

In this new situation, Mário assumed a completely passive attitude, excluding himself, lying down, hunched up on the couch and sometimes covering his head with a cushion. There was a clear indication that he felt the task should be left to me and his mother. In the first joint sessions with the mother he also displayed a physical movement that involved his sliding down from the couch, resembling a baby who slips down and tries to climb back up. The mother's participation lasted for six months (from November 1981 to May 1982), and during this period she remembered facts and events, was emotionally moved, brought photographs at my request, and reviewed as far as she could her relationship with this first child. She was, however, unable to go very far with this and to really think about what it meant to have a child like Mário, how she felt about this experience. Her imagination seemed to be locked against it, resorting to non-verbal appeals for help.

Mário's exclusion of himself from these joint sessions took the form of his refusal to initiate and participate in the conversation. I had the opportunity to get a more complete overview of his development, one in which the mother appeared as being careful to discourage her baby from forming bad habits, such as wanting to be picked up all the time, or going to sleep with his mother – generally everything that required more of the mother's presence. These rules apparently avoided emotional contact with the baby, a situation that probably caused her intense anxiety. She tried to be "very objective", an attitude that seemed to me to diminish contact with her own psychic reality, her own imagination, and therefore with her baby, too. When she referred to certain recent features of Mário's behaviour – for example, not asking for her when he is ill, demanding company or other things, she does not make the link between his attitude and the kind of relationship she established when he was a baby. I tried to mobilise the mother's resources for bonding with other aspects of Mário that had been paralysed owing to such a debilitating view of his "symptoms". And in fact, after some sessions, the mother reported that Mário had started to ask for things – for example, a dog, which he was then given. He began playing games with his mother, covering her eyes and asking her to guess who it is, and only letting her go when she says his name.

As regards Mário's storytelling, the mother was unable to remember accurately when this behaviour began, but stated that he would ask her to tell him stories everyday, from before he learned to read. He would then also browse through magazines with her, looking for subjects in the index, reading the titles of the pieces and holding onto the magazine, leafing through it repetitively. According to his mother, the stories that he invents and tells by himself are related to his current experiences. She notices that he is ultra-methodical, follows a rigid schedule and is compulsive in his use of the stories. He will often tell her: "Now we are going home to do my little things" – an activity that consists of going into his room or the office and staying there talking to himself, grasping a tape measure or a plastic string. He invariably interrupts his talking when the mother enters the room and wants her to go away quickly so that he can resume his activities.

During the period in which the mother took part in the sessions, Mário intensified his reporter-speaker-actor broadcastings and reacted to my comments regarding what he is actually saying and what he could be feeling by hitting me, talking over me, listening to me and then laughing at my interpretations, or, as a last resort, stopping talking and lying down with his head covered by the cushion.

This new exploration again led me to think of a mismatch in the mother–baby relationship (with factors coming from both) that contributed strongly to the construction of an object-with-no-inside in Mário's mind. Although the mother had made no mention of post-partum depression, she seemed to me in a mixed state of depression and feeling threatened. I have never seen her smile and it is difficult to imagine her "dreaming" of her baby, while she performs the required physical ministrations. Applying Bion's concept of maternal *reverie,* one concludes that in the case of an autistic child the tragedy that took place was a failure of the primal dependent relationship. The failure of the container function of the external object (as a result of a primitive sensuality, desire for fusion and great possessiveness) can lead to the failure of the concept of a container *self.*

Mário's storytelling activity, as recounted by the parents and as shown during the sessions, forms a substitute for play. Children use toys as instruments for fantasy and thinking, but Mário would never be able to play in this manner. Mário's toys are words. For him, words are things and not representations of them, showing a failure in symbol-formation.

I also believe that storytelling for Mário constitutes pathological self-containment. The development of a "second skin" (Bick), in which dependency is replaced by pseudo-independency, as demonstrated in Mário's "reporter-speaker" behaviour, protects him from abandonment, but arrests his development because it obstructs the interchange of the necessary projections and introjections. In these circumstances, the use of projective identification to exercise omnipotent control is a pre-condition for the object relationship.

I will recount one of the sessions participated in by Mário's mother.

Session of February 25th, 1982

When I call Mário, he is in the toilet and the mother comes in and sits down. I ask her how their holidays were and the mother comments that during the holidays it is hard for him because he is inactive. In fact he went to spend a week with his brother at his cousins' home and felt well there; he played with them and participated in their activities. But when the cousins came to spend a week with them, Mário stayed in his little world, "in the cloister", and did not play. During this past week, she insisted on him going for a walk every day to do something, as "otherwise he becomes aggressive". He would go out, but come back soon after.

"Yesterday", she continues, "he stayed up with us watching TV until midnight, but he wakes up early, even when it is unnecessary, because he enjoys watching the news at half past seven on the TV."

I suggest that Mário might be interested in doing something together with his father, which surprises the mother.

Since entering, he has lain down with the cushion over his head, demonstrating that he is unwilling to listen, to take part. However, his mood toward me is friendly. When I ask him whether school has started, he does not reply, as if he had established a rule for not talking or participating while the mother is in the room. Still, he seems interested in maintaining a good relationship with me, and so gets up, opens the box, gets a piece of paper, writes down something and throws it, keeping his back to me and the mother. As such, he maintains his attitude of not talking, indicating that if I really am interested then I must make the effort to find out what he wrote, which was: "Classes will start on Monday."

Almost at the end of the session, the mother comments that he was very interested in coming back to therapy; that on the previous day he reminded her that he had therapy the next day, and during the session he keeps talking about those races and classifications. She exclaims: "He doesn't give that a rest, even on the first day!"

She tells me about the academic plan they have this year for Mário. I stress the importance of practical learning and career orientation for Mário, as he will be finishing elementary school this year and going onto secondary education next year. I explain to the mother that it is necessary to establish Mário in learning some practical activity that will give him the opportunity for longer contact with external reality in order to stimulate him and avoid inactivity, thus trying to counteract his tendency to become cloistered.

The mother is interested and says she will search for sources of information. CIAM offers various technical programmes.

I ask Mário how we should proceed next week – if he wants to come alone on Monday.

Mário: I do.

Analyst: And what about your mother's presence in the sessions?

He shows me two fingers.

Analyst: Which sessions?

He writes down that his are on Mondays and Thursdays, whilst Tuesdays and Wednesdays would be together with his mother. We agree to try this schedule.

Meanwhile the mother gave me more details about Mário's home life. (At this period she also brought me a written account of Mário's history.) She told me that her husband sometimes has violent outbursts and lashes out at people. Later, he regrets his behaviour, but everyone becomes afraid of him – it is a potential minefield. Mário has never asked for him when going to bed. His mother used to put him in his cot and then leave. He would take some time to fall asleep and usually he would remove everything from the cot, remaining on the bare mattress. But he neither cried nor called for his mother. Until he was three and half years old, if he were lying down, even awake, he would not go to the toilet, but would defaecate or urinate in the bed. He also remained in bed when awake if his mother was still sleeping. His brother, however, would go to the parents' bed or call his mother for attention from his room. Mário has never called for his mother or asked for company.

On the day he was bitten by a dog, three years ago, he spent the night awake and with his eyes open; his mother went to see him but he neither complained nor asked her to stay. The mother was deeply moved when relating this. Mário also tended not to complain of pain, fever or influenza; this only started to happen two or three years ago.

In general, and with the exception of *Placar* (a football magazine, which he asks for on Tuesdays) and sweets, he tends not to ask for anything. However, recently he asked for a winter coat and a pair of boots, and was also quite insistent about getting a new dog, as the old one died. The mother was against the idea, as it would require a lot of looking after and it makes the lawn smell. Moreover, Mário will not walk it, even on a leash. He has now promised the mother that he will look after it and has asked for a puppy as his Christmas present.

Mário's mother began potty training him at the age of nine months, sitting him on the potty when she changed his nappy. When he was one year old, she would leave him nappyless if it was hot. Until he was about three, he would sometimes ask to go; later (before he could speak) he would pull on his mother's hand for her to take him to the toilet.

It should be noted that, although the mother's participation in the sessions yielded more material and provided her with a space in which to be heard and where some of her questions could be answered, it did not seem to contribute to progress in her relationship with Mário.

Feelings of intolerance – how to proceed?

My feelings of intolerance, as Meltzer said, occupy the place of the broken-down child: the feeling that nothing can be done to change Mário's condition as his opposition to change is extraordinarily strong. These feelings increased significantly and I told Mário, in a session at the beginning of 1982, that I was presented with someone who didn't want to make any contact, who insisted on maintaining the status quo, and would not accept interference from anyone. I suggested he review what he really expected from the sessions and I asked for his cooperation, because otherwise we would be unable to work together. His reply was that he would like to think about it next year. So I based my ensuing work with him on this hint of interest and availability. I aimed towards creating space for me in our relationship and achieving the right to manifest my presence. It is possible however that, through this attitude, I was taking on the role of baby-Mário that he imposed on me in every session and that he could control by acting out the role of a tyrannical parent.

I began to demonstrate dramatically that his uninterrupted storytelling, which prevents him from listening to me, is a way of expelling me: to show this I head for the exit. He stops me and leads me back to my chair. In this way he "recaptures" me, leaving me on the chair while he continues with his stories. Then I get up again, and we go on repeating these movements, until an opportunity to speak and listen arises. Little by little, his furious reaction to my questioning becomes less intense.

To give another example of my feelings of intolerance: in July 1982, I asked myself whether this relationship was indeed analytical or if I was simply playing the role of a babysitter. Was I obstinately trying to repair the irreparable? Four and a half years trying to develop a nourishing relationship with him, and he continues to refuse it? It was then that I told him it was impossible for me to continue his analysis as he was refusing to establish contact with me, and this showed he wanted nothing to do with baby Mário. He said he did not want to stop. He asked whether I wanted to get rid of him and concluded by saying that what I was telling him was just a piece of theatre. I explained that my attitude was not theatrical but real, but that for him I was only real when I was baby Mário. I always had to listen to him and hold him so he could not kick me.

The following week he refrained from being a reporter. He began the session by greeting me, lying down and covering his head with the cushion that he usually holds when being a reporter. He seemed to be very worried and his eyes were full of tears. I told him that this was his reply: not to be the reporter-speaker so that he was not sent away or, in other words, that he was trying in his way to help the analysis by keeping me on his side.

Meltzer's comment: There is a place in technique for indicating to the patient that no progress is being made, and that progress is a condition for you being able to continue the work responsibly, since your aim is therapy is not babysitting (see my paper on "An interruption technique" for dealing with the analytic impasse, which I think was published in the Argentine *Revista* in about 1975 [Meltzer 1968, in English]). But I do not think that a young therapist is in a position to use such a technique because his method and skills are still so undeveloped that he must rely on supervisors and their experience. Nonetheless, one can get to the end of one's tether and you may indicate that your patience and tolerance seem to be coming to an end. This is in effect what you have done, and in this way have challenged the part of Mário that is attached to you to abandon its passive position, non-partisan as it were, and to come out clearly in your favour against the "critic-reporter". But, on the other hand, the material dries up, and you do not then have the means of bonding Mário to your way of thinking; rather, the emotional-erotic infantile attachment (as demonstrated by his weeping posture on the couch). You need the material from the reporter in order to fight against his influence over Mário's mind.

Here is perfectly good material to approach in any way your imagination leads your interest, keeping always in mind the underlying theme: that he cannot bear being merely an outsider, merely a spectator of the world of adult sexuality, and instead has posted himself as the commentator on adolescent competitive sexuality.

You could take up the geography in terms of the orifices of the female body. You could approach the problem of his expectation that the female is just a prize to be won and always yields herself as a possession to the winner, etc.; i.e. his misconceptions of the mysteries of femininity. You could take up the problem of the cold depression, feminine frigidity, male impotence, the absence of tender feelings, in his conception of sexuality.

But never lose sight of the primary object of masturbation, the basic stupidity of the know-it-all critic part of himself.

Synthesis

In August 1982, when Mário was sixteen, I wrote to Dr Meltzer giving a synthesis of the analytic process with Mário over the past four years, with his four weekly sessions. I gave a recap of his history from his untreated autism at age two: how he only began to speak at age five; and how his brother (three years younger), according to his parents, helped to "bring him to life". I wrote:

> During the sessions, Mário talks constantly, about sports, the news, world events or television shows, and dramatizes them by enacting the role of a commentator, reporter or actor. He enters fully into these dramatizations and, in addition to not tolerating interruptions, only finishes when the hour is practically up.
>
> I presume that this incessant talking is what Tustin calls the autistic object, which serves to prevent the perception of a separate identity, ensuring through sensorial qualities that the object is always present. It is talk that does not serve to communicate, but rather to avoid contact with me, so he can withdraw into his stories. Nevertheless this talking, combined with his behaviour, constitutes material that

provides a form of access to him, as you said in your previous comments.

However, the "technical problem" (to give it a name) is that he refuses to enter into contact with and to listen to me. I understand his fear of contact and the reversal he carries out in his relationship with me – he is the breast that feeds me. I am a mouth-ear. If I talk to him showing that I am thinking of him and can reach him, it provokes his rage. Could it be due to the threat of breaking the illusion of continuity and control?

Over these four years of analysis, I have put into practice various strategies in an effort to reach him. In the beginning, I analysed his relationship with me, the function he attributed to me, the place he set out for me. He seemed not to hear me. I also told him that he was prevented from listening to me by his great fear of entering into contact with me and realising his situation.

After your supervision, I began to interpret the content of what he said. In my third phase, I noticed just how addicted he is to using his stories (autistic objects) and I decided to fight against them, even though this seemed to me to be a position diametrically opposed to an analytic one, which does not "fight against" (which is a feature of the "desire to cure"), but rather analyses.

In my fourth phase, my belief in how analytic work should proceed prevailed and, faced with someone who wants no contact, who wants to remain as he is, nobody has the right to do anything about it. I explained these thoughts to him so that he could review his initiative in coming to analysis and asked for his collaboration, as otherwise it would be impossible for us to work together. He replied that he would like to leave thinking about this until the following year. I worked with this sign of interest and willingness in every session thereafter. Worked in the sense of obtaining "the necessary space and rights of existence and presence" for myself in a field in which he felt himself to be the sole owner and tyrant. Acting in this way, I was perhaps taking on the role of an anti-tyrant, or rather, that of the baby that he deposited in me at each session and which was controlled and suffocated by a tyrant-mother who took away the right to existence and identity – who took away the baby's creativeness.

In January of 1982 I also experimented by asking the mother to participate in one of the weekly sessions so that I could observe the relationship between them. Mário stayed quiet during these sessions, listening and always refusing to participate, leaving his mother and me to conduct the session. I abandoned this approach after a few months, having come to the conclusion that it did not seem particularly useful. I am currently pursuing a more "active" analytic attitude in the sense of also having the right to speak, and, if I am not listened to or if my presence is denied strongly, I get up and threaten to leave the room, at which point Mário will get up and lead me back to my seat. He then continues with his stories and, shortly afterwards, I will get up again, heading for the door, until something new happens. His rage at being interrupted has significantly lessened and there have been fewer manifestations of physical aggression against me.

Meltzer's comment: It is a good rule to assume that if the patient comes to the session, some contact exists. No one, not even a small child, can be forced totally against his will, to make contact, to remain in your presence, to communicate. The problem from the structural point of view is always to first try to discover the organization of the personality that is representing itself.

Between the ages of ten to fifteen, when children feel they are in the no-man's land of being neither children (irresponsible) nor adult (having some prerogatives, freedom and privacy) their position vis-à-vis the world is often dominated by a destructive part, a pseudo-superegoist critic who watches, observes and criticizes the adult world and longs to join the adolescent community which it envisages as pushing the adults into the rubbish bin and taking over the world of wealth, beauty and sexuality. This know-it-all critic, especially in intelligent and verbal children,

presents itself to the therapist in defiance, flaunting its domin-
ion over the child's inner world and attitudes. My technique is
to challenge it in a spirit of adamant good-humour to a test of
the validity of its evidence, modes of thought, use of language,
knowledge, logic and capacity for imagination. The latter is, in a
way, the most important, for its omniscience is in fact a manifestation of the poverty of its imagination, that is, its inability to see
more than one possible construction to be put on any situation.

You have always, I think, underestimated his attachment to
you and the value he placed on your interest, perseverance, tolerance to his projections of mental pain – and probably also underestimated his erotic interest. However, being at an early stage in
your development, it is important that you should feel free to try
different approaches to the material (that is, the phenomenon)
that the patient presents to you, but in the interest of *exploration*
and not of *control*.

Any behaviour by a patient which a) is not physically dangerous to patient or analyst; b) stays within the geographical limits
that make the analyst's work possible; and c) does not interfere
with the rights of any other patient – is fundamentally accept-
able for analytic scrutiny.

Meltzer's reply was, therefore, that Mário's desire to continue
the analysis is evidence that, gradually and silently, a relationship
between the baby Mário and analyst-mother is being built, in
which he shows his attachment and appreciation of my perseverance, interest and tolerance for the projection of his mental
pain. For a moment the patient contained the analyst. And his
insistent desire that I feel, in the countertransference, what it is
like to be with a mother who does allow contact or nurture, a
mother-radio-TV, is perhaps due to a belief that I do not know
how terrible it is to be in such a situation.

Bion's work in developing Klein's understanding of the projective identification not only emphasized the importance of the
analyst's capacity for containing the patient's projections (or the
mother's regarding the child), but also resulted in the progressive
attention given to very primitive preverbal communication.

My actions showed Mário that my resources were now coming to an end as I was unable to establish contact with him through my interpretations. The hopelessness that I could feel increasing due to not being heard is Mário's primitive communication, identified with the mother-speaker, an object constructed in his mind that protects him from the pain caused by the interpretations.

It is useless to accuse him of making me feel excluded or to show that he feels excluded. What is needed is a way of getting across to him that I do understand something of how it feels to have as internal object a mother that does not respond to his feelings. And I need the ability to bear this experience as well as his resentment about it.

Attempts at "translation"

After coming to understand my situation better regarding the transference-countertransference, I undertook a new task: how to use the reporter-speaker's material? How to translate the "Márioguese" into Portuguese: that is, how to start from his code without superimposing another, verbalizing his emotions and mental states?

After my threat to terminate the analysis, he became quiet and silent, lying down on the couch, covering his head, eyeing me occasionally and then retreating into himself. I say: "Now you are a baby like you think I want you to be, an autistic baby…".

In a session in June of 1982, he commented on temperatures: "Now we are going to talk about the temperatures in February: hot! Here, now, 30°C. In Brasília, the hot weather is coming on strongly, with lower temperatures forecast for between 11 pm and 7 in the morning. A minimum of 30°C and maximum of 34°C. Here, now, we have 20°C." I interject: "Listen! We're carrying on our lessons in Márioguese: when he says 'temperature' he means 'emotion', etc'." Mário laughs at my intervention.

In October of 1982, the father came to four consecutive weekly sessions, having missed the first due to an unavoidable work appointment. Mário took on his father's place, writing down the youth football championship scores. In these interviews, the father asks him to sit, instead of lying down like he did when the mother was present; he acquiesced in some of his father's requests, but without speaking, using only gestures or writing down replies and throwing them with his back to us, as if to say: "If you want an answer, you can go to the bother of getting it." The father communicates something new: Mário "is getting used to his mother pandering to his whims, and he allows only her to look after him – never asking anything of me, even when I am there and nearer to him than his mother." His free time at home is dedicated to doing his "little things" in the office, where he stays writing or talking out loud.

Following the sessions with his father, we tried some sessions with his brother. Mário agreed, I think, as part of accepting my work and my investigations about himself.

After this I then promised Mário to spend some time with him on a "task" in which I would enter unconditionally into his world of numbers and lists, undertaking a genuine participation and interest in whatever topic he wished to develop – leaving interpretations for later in the session. This allowed us to establish contact through the medium of his own utterly eccentric world. I became an attentive collaborator in his "inventions". When he did not accept my participation and distanced himself from me, I took the attitude of someone who was also busy, doing a task of my own – for instance, playing a game in which one has to list the names of towns, fruits, animals, colours, objects, rivers and football teams that begin with a certain letter, and asking for his help in coming up with answers. He would normally approach me and show an interest. This was one of the ways I attempted to increase the points of actual contact between us.

After the period of experimentation with his family, Mário began his sessions with long lists of candidates for governor, state representative, congressman, city councillor and senator – a topical subject in Brazil due to the coming elections of November 15th, 1982, albeit a theme that already existed in our relationship. The question was, who among his relatives would win me? It should be made clear that an intervention such as this, which may even be correct in its transference dynamics, did not alter his "need" to carry on creating this long list until he decided it was completed. Fully immersed in reading it out he would simply inform me (if at all) which point he had got to: thus, "I am at number 1723... almost finishing the state representatives...", or "Now I am going to start on candidates in list 4", or "I think that I will be able to finish the list in the last session" (in this last example, he is referring to the last session of the year before the holidays that begin on December 15th, 1982).

I tell him that this is his way of organizing the disorganization I caused with all my manoeuvres when trying to find a way to enter into contact with him and to overcome his attempts to alienate himself from contact; but that he is constantly informing me of what he is doing and at what stage he is at, so that I can wait for him.

Meltzer's comment: The description of the analytic situation seems to emphasize, first, the concrete, acted-in-the-transference modality and, second, the state of the relationship to the object (internal, primarily) of what Winnicott called "being alone in the presence of the mother." He considered this a very good name, whereas I am inclined to see it as obsessive, controlling, sadistic and denigrating. It treats the analyst-mother as an inanimate object, a toilet, and is solely preoccupied with the world of men. In this case, it is also essentially a hierarchic structure of authority (tyranny) and may imply a basic assumption type of mindless obedience to group dynamics.

I would not use the term "autistic" for the present state, although this degree of obsession is, as we described, characteristic of the post-autistic organization with its two-dimensionality, which I now recognize as strangely related to the involvement in the group mentality of the basic assumption. The involvement of other members is an interesting experiment in combining analysis and family therapy, but it also so complicates the transference as to make it extremely difficult to follow it in any detail.

CHAPTER FIVE

Mário reaches adolescence

It is now February, 1983. Our sessions continue after a six weeks' holiday. At the beginning of the year he continues with his list of candidates, which takes about two months to complete and runs to around 58 pages. The sense I make of this "great invention" is that of a manoeuvre that will infallibly maintain neutrality in the face of the threat of my attempts at "anti-neutrality". I believe this is the only way he can be with me. If I threaten to get up and leave (fighting against his mental customs), he gets up and leads me from the door back to my seat, asking me to stay. However his use of autistic manoeuvres has somewhat decreased. It seems we have reached a modus vivendi in which he feels bonded to me, does not dismiss me, and is more often able to listen to me.

Session of February 10th, 1983

As soon as he enters, Mário starts to draw up a calendar for 1983.

Analyst: Strange child. Now we're getting a 1983 calendar. This is too much!

Mário continues as if nothing had happened.

Analyst: This is impossible! I shall have to leave. (*I get up.*)

Mário: No way are you leaving!

He gets up, grabs my arm, leads me back to my seat and then carries on drawing up the calendar.

Analyst: Let's do this: I shall be Mário and you shall be Marisa. You sit here and I'll sit there.

Mário accepts the game and goes to my seat, reclining almost all the way back before putting his feet up on the table, but removing them when I complain. He closes his eyes, pretending to sleep, and snores loudly. Then he looks for me at the other end of the table, groping around with his arms and legs. He gets up, eyes closed, and walks around, hands stretched out in front of him, touching the table, couch, walls, doors, the sink… until he arrives in front of me (I am seated at the other end of the table). He turns back to the couch and lies down on it. I note that he became agitated with this change of roles. In my seat, I am writing down the days and months of the year, just as he was.

Mário gets up from the couch and takes an old magazine from a closet. He leafs through it, stopping to look at pictures of scantily clad women, but does so without any change in expression.

Meltzer's comment: The technique of role reversal in play is something children initiate themselves, in fact there is probably an important element of reversal in the whole obsessive spectrum, reversing the (independent parent–helpless baby) relation. When you reverse it again, it seems to be transformed into a situation of light-dark, sighted-blind, erotic-impassive, and dualities, having a reference to the discontinuity of the baby's experience of the parents in the night and during the day. What this perhaps implies in the usual situation with Mário might well be mother, being ignored, controlled and denigrated by the baby, thinking only of when the baby will fall asleep so that she can go to daddy and get a new, better baby (patient).

Session of February 17th 1983

It is the Thursday after the Carnival holidays.

Mário: Tomorrow it's at 9:45, isn't it? *(Referring to the time of a replacement session, scheduled for Friday.)*

Analyst: Yes.

Mário *(shaking my hand)*: Ah! Well, good morning. Turn on the fan, it's hot in here.

Analyst: Heat – the emotion at meeting again after so many days.

Mário smiles and continues listing the youth football championship results.

Analyst: I notice that Italy lost and was eliminated from this championship you are making up. Italy is Marisa, while Brazil-Mário is winning. You are disguising the competition, hiding how you are fixing things.

Mário *(laughs)*: Ha! Ha! Ha!

Analyst: I see how you want to beat me. To be the best. By knowing everything, you cut me out. But sometimes, you think I am better and you want to learn from me.

Mário feels he has been found out, and tries to explain that Italy does take part, etc., but he ends up changing the subject and continues writing another list that he had begun earlier ("January", etc.), until the end of the session.

Meltzer's comment: Here, the preoccupation with winning is not a manifestation of Oedipal competitiveness, but of struggle for status in the hierarchical structure - i.e. a question of survival. Clearly, it is a jungle, a concentration camp kind of place where the weak are put up against the wall (and shot) and the strong and ruthless survive. But who are the monsters, the guards, the architects of this claustrophobic situation? His sadistic laugh in response to your recognition of his structure and devious ways clearly indicates that he is the architect of this game of life and death.

Session of February 24th, 1983

Mário walks in and, opening the box as he has for several months, removes some paper and a pen (now, always a red one) and writes: "Brazilian State Championship: First Phase – Group Draw."

I tell him he is grouping, perhaps due to his need to put everything in order for the weekend – Mário and Marisa in their own respective group or family.

Mário: Look what happened to the São Paulo team!
Analyst: What?
Mário: In the Western Group, along with Mato Grosso and Mato Grosso do Sul. (*He continues writing.*)
Mário: Right, now that all the groups have been drawn, the matches will begin… In the second phase, there are two teams in each group. Look where the São Paulo team is now.

(He shows me the sheet of paper.)

Mário: They will play Rio Grande do Sul, in two legs: first at home, at Morumbi Stadium, and then away, in Porto Alegre.

Today, he is talking to me spontaneously, letting me know what he is doing. The games are in the future but he already knows the results, because he controls it all; which makes us think that he is referring to the arrangements of his internal objects.

Meltzer's comment: Now he seems quite clearly to move into the position of a cruel God who allows little human creatures to think that they have free will and can achieve their hearts' desires through work, intelligence, cooperation, knowledge, etc. But, in reality, this savage God has planned everything in advance: crushing some, leaving them in despair just when they think they have succeeded, destroying others through insanity brought about by triumph. This is the baby's picture of the parents' relation to the children, making them manic with attention and interest in the day and crushing them with isolation, neglect and betrayal (making a new baby) at night.

Session of March 7th, 1983

Mário is sad and depressed. He looks at me and his eyes fill with tears. He stands there, a piece of paper and a red pen in hand, thoughtful. I describe to him how he seems to me. He begins a sequence of numbers in decreasing order, and after each new line he begins with the same numbers, less one:

81-82-83-84-85-86-87-88-89-90
80-81-82-83-84-85-86-87-88-89
79-78, etc.

I note that he wrote the same sequence last Monday and I tell him it seems to me to be the path the he mentally creates to bring himself back to me. I associate this with a drawing he made in November 1982, when I had asked him and his brother to do some drawings. His drawing began from the centre, spiralling out before returning back to the centre.

While he writes he makes faces, contorting his mouth, showing conflicting emotions of resentment and hate and weeping-sadness for me, all the while following his numeric route, really making it seem that this allows him to experience these emotions, possibly arising from the weekend separation, and to re-establish contact with me. The atmosphere pervading the session is one of depression. He starts to move about when he finishes his decreasing sequence of numbers – the session has almost ended.

Meltzer's comment: The story continues: during the day, with all the interest, attention and food received from mother, the baby feels that it is growing bigger and more important every moment of every hour. But when he wakes up the next morning, he finds that something has grown smaller, not larger. What can it be? The number of days left to him as the baby. For the "writing is on the wall": t a new baby will soon replace him and he will feel that he has wasted so much of his time with you in an illusion of absolute possession and control of you that he did not notice how precious you (the breast) were to him. Now he can see the beauty and goodness but it is too late! He used to assume that time was circular (the spiral) but now he sees it is linear and uni-directional.

Mário comes in and gets the sheets of paper to continue his list of the regions of Brazil. I stand up and he, very alert, rises up, saying: "No! You aren't leaving?" He holds onto my arm whilst remaining on his feet, reading his list and telling me that it will only take a little longer before he is finished. I tell him that as long as he writes this list, he is excluding me and all I can do is leave. He commands me to be quiet and sit down in my place, because he "wants me to", but continues with the list. I tell him that as long as he continues to cling onto his inventions, there is no room for me, and I get up again. Mário grabs me, leads me away from the door and stands in front of me, saying "Only over my dead body." I then pretend that I am going to shoot him, and walk over his sheet of paper with the list of Brazil's regions. There is the beginning of a struggle; he is irritated by my firm determination, for as soon as he returns to his list I try to open the door and leave the room. He hits me with the cushion and tries to get the upper hand by standing on the table, threatening me, trying to frighten me.

Analyst: It's no use, Mário. The reason I carry on is the possibility of your giving up your bad habits and relating to me.

He has already returned to his list. An incredible compulsion. Again, I try to leave and, again, he grabs me.

Mário: You can do whatever you like here, except leave.

Analyst: I just want to continue with your analysis.

Mário: You are in jail. You've served five years and there are three, or perhaps one more, years to go. Last year, I let you out on parole, but you didn't know how to make the most of it. You have to stay in jail.

Analyst: What did I do to deserve this sentence?

Mário: You murdered a child and now have to serve your sentence.

This exchange has been accompanied by physical struggles and cushion strikes throughout.

Mário: It's in the back of the van with you.

Analyst: As if I were another of your poohs. You want to lock me up in your behind.

Mário (laughing): That's right, that's where you should go, all tied up. Obey me or I'll kill you.

Analyst: I can see your resentment and sadism toward me. You see me as a murderous mother and think I should be imprisoned in your bottom, like one of your poohs.

Mário: You will only be freed if you behave well. Three years from now. This began in March 1977, and will only end in March 1986.

I am completely involved in the dramatic action and am astonished at Mário's revelation, for now I am the villain, the murderer "running loose" in the stories that he told. Now I have consistency and perhaps something to work with in the relationship.

Meltzer's comment: You have clearly picked up the central theme of the drama, that you want a new baby when this one is so cruel to you, but behind this obsessive drama there are also the facts of life, uni-directional time and the limit of every relationship which is good and therefore growth-promoting. This latter theme, being the primary anxiety, defending against the obsession which generates secondary anxiety, is more important to stress – i.e. he cannot bear his good-baby relationship with you because of the inevitability of weaning (death of the breast). In the obsessive defensive system, it is the baby's death ("over my dead body") that is the price of the mother's freedom; if you only pay attention to being kept in jail and not to the psychic reality it defends against you, offering him no alternative system, only a reversal: you in control, he in jail. The alternative means change, growth and ending. The depressive position.

For two weeks we have been playing "Hangman". One person thinks of a word and writes dashes corresponding to the number of letters in the word. The opponent then has to guess letters until the word is filled in, but is only allowed ten wrong guesses, as after each wrong guess a stroke is added to a drawing that will eventually depict a person hanging from the scaffold.

Shrewd players can use certain tactics that make it easier, for example, going through the vowels first. In Portuguese, certain double consonants are common and these can be identified by examining the spaces between the vowels. So it is not simply a random guessing game, it is also one in which the opponent needs to imagine the possible combinations.

Meltzer's comment: As with so many children's games, this can be interpreted at the infantile level as a game about weaning: whether the "end" of the feeding game is to be experienced as a persecution and punishment or a success, which nonetheless is a cause for grief due to relinquishment of the "old" breast (which will become "young" again for the next baby). The "mistakes" are those of action-without-thought, based on sensuality, greed, competitiveness and cruelty toward the mother and her inside-babies. The "success" is based on understanding the mind of the other, both mother (analyst) understanding baby (patient) and baby (patient) understanding mother (analyst).

Life Prospects

For the past two years, Mário has been participating in group sporting activities at the Community Centre, after a suggestion I made in a conversation with his parents. I advised the parents, on several occasions, to provide him with the means to expand his areas of interest and even enrol him in an apprenticeship that would suit his character and preferences. As regards his career, I suggested making use of his (obsessive) defences, albeit without protecting him from having to face any new situations.

We reduced the number of weekly sessions to three in order to enable him to attend a typing course, three mornings per week.

Mário's sensitivity to the changes in the setting-container is noticeable. His fear of annihilation, of the state of non-integration, is more evident and his second skin defences (Bick) are more pronounced: that is, he again spends long periods occupying himself with his stories and lists, without leaving any gaps for his real self to slip through. His capacity for self-restraint through the introjection of a living container object is very unstable and it gets completely lost as a result of these changes in the movements of the container-analyst. This corroborates with what we stated previously: the problem for post-autistics is the failure to achieve a stable internal mental space where his or her object can safely reside. At the least provocation, the memory of Mário's object is expelled, forcing him to resort to the use of present and concrete container objects (i.e. non mental ones), as in his continuous talking.

Mário's mental condition means that absence cannot be experienced other than through the threat of annihilation. Therefore mental functioning cannot develop and symbolic activity does not progress; introjections and projections happen slowly and only during moments of exceptionally stable container conditions with a low level of frustration and anxiety. The danger of mental functioning deteriorating owing to rigidity is very pronounced.

Mário is aware of his difficulties to some extent: "I do not know if I can enrol in the army with my condition." He also knows that he has improved thanks to his analysis: "I was out of my mind when I lifted you off the ground with my eyes alone" (a reference to a time when he tried to lift the chair I was sitting on with his feet).

Together, we agreed on a date to stop the analysis, in six months' time.

In the final interviews with Mário and his parents, they say that he has significantly improved as regards making contact, taking the initiative, and in expressing his feelings and preferences. They used to think that it was wonderful when he recited all the capitals of the world, but they now recognize it was a negative sign, and things are better now because he participates by talking to people.

I point out that being in emotional contact is the opposite of using defences (such as talking to himself) against the new, the unknown. On the other hand Mário's attitude to his daily routine and commitments is to stick to established schedules and avoid unexpected changes, postponements, etc. This attitude – his scheduling – must be resisted; it must not simply be accepted, but rather discussed so that he can be open to seeing alternatives.

I summarize below the results of two Rorschach tests: one from when he was eleven and a half years old (prior to being referred to me) and the other from age fifteen. We can see that Mário lived in a completely delirious and magical world, had a very inflated ego that was vulnerable to attack and that occupied all the room in his mind; his experience of life was chaotic and invaded by sensuous feelings. This sensuality diminished and he became more solid, more contained, able to endure internal tension for longer without demanding its immediate release, instead making some attempt at communication. However, this came at the expense of structuring defences and limiting his affection and interests.

The Rorschach test taken at age eleven and a half

This test indicated that Mário's power of reasoning was badly affected by the severity of his emotional problems. He showed extreme subjectivity; his relationships were random and at times absurd; he was incapable of following a coherent line of thought, confusing the accidental with the essential and fantasy with reality. It was impossible for him to learn through experience. He paid more attention to form than to meaning and factual content. This was his only mechanism of organization and the only way he could avoid being invaded by feelings he could not control.

At the heart of his condition was a diminished capacity for feeling anxiety; that is, he was rarely moved by feelings of anxiety to find ways of solving it. On the contrary, he did not internalize human values and parameters of affection. A feeling of empti-ness and the destitution of interpersonal bonds predominated. He only became upset when there was a risk of being invaded and attacked. He sought compensation in substitute objects as he lacked the discrimination to recognize he was feeling unloved and without a sense of belonging.

Mário had to rely entirely on others for his psychic balance. He had a very fragile ego and a marked poverty of adaptive and defensive mechanisms; he demonstrated a lack of affective containment, a lot of impulsiveness and a disproportion between stimulus and response, because he lacked any judgement of context and opportunity. There was also no clear distinction between internal and external worlds. He had a tendency to select morbid and destructive aspects in the environment and in himself. He was liable to have uncontrolled phobic or panic reactions, for he could neither establish the nature of objects, nor determine the quality of the stimuli which entered his consciousness.

These were the reasons why Mário displayed marked inse-curity, excessive dependency on others, limited self-criticism and introspective capacity and exacerbated sensitivity to sensual stimuli. His ways of relating to others and acquiring knowledge depended on sensory reactions that were not logically organized but followed magical, subjective rules. It was thought possible that there could also be a neurological problem that contributed to decreasing both his ability to integrate and his resistance to frustration.

The Rorschach test taken at age fifteen

This test was taken in the fourth year of analysis. What is noticeable is that Mário *a priori* established a method of work-ing entirely arbitrarily: he deemed it appropriate to give three answers per inkblot image. This allowed him to soften and annul any emotional impact the images could cause him, or any aspects he felt unprepared to deal with. His idiosyncratic approach therefore followed no logical criteria; on the contrary, it seemed much more linked to the mythical content of the number 3.

Another feature was that the answers he gave were partial, sometimes insignificant or even absurd. Some kind of childish reasoning was dominant in which he would take the parts for the whole. He demonstrated some contact with reality, mainly through stereotype and rigidity. Evidently, he lacked the capacity to be informed by objective data, had no aptitude for reasoning, and his conclusions were biased and "manic". He showed no awareness of this.

There was confusion between the internal and external worlds, and his consciousness was constantly invaded by primitive psychic processes and magical rituals for holding threatening fantasies at bay. These fantasies had a strong destructive content – could he be afraid of being devoured, or of destroying the other with his excrement?

The conclusion was that Mário has no clear notion of identity and of the particular features he may possess as a person and individual. What most disorganizes him are his feelings of aggression and envy. Usually, he deals with these by minimising them through denial and projective identification. What is noticeable is an extremely primitive level of organization whereby he does not even recognize all his body parts as belonging to him, much less the feelings that he fears. Furthermore, he is very pressured by a dangerous and feminine superego. A state of emotional excitability and heightened susceptibility to affective stimuli predominates in him.

In such circumstances, he withdraws too much, clearly demonstrating an exacerbated sensuality, and losing sight of context and proportion. He lacks internalized models of constructive emotional relationships and can only imagine tyrannical or parasitic bonds. It seems that he has never truly established object relations; on the contrary, he has substituted these with highly dangerous myths and ghosts. Because of this, he feels overly persecuted and threatened, full of fantasies of death and destruction. In an attempt to find stability, he tends to deprive his objects of interest of life, resulting in a marked internal aridity and indifference to contact that is a far cry from expressing what he really feels.

CHAPTER SIX

Review

In July 1997, eighteen years after the end of Mário's analysis, I reviewed the case with Meltzer in a supervision group at Oxford, which also included José Americo Junqueira, João Carlos Braga, and Marli Braga. After reading out the introductory sections, the first meetings, and the session of August 15th, 1979 [page 23, above], Dr Meltzer commented:

Meltzer: It certainly reminds me (and probably at that time reminded me) of a boy we had in Oxford who was in the process of progressing from being autistic and mute to gradually becoming more and more schizophrenic. He also had these very elaborate, quasi-historical stories that he made up, which were really confabulated but had their roots in history and Bible stories and things of this sort. This boy was more particularly rooted in the Old Testament and the story of Abraham and Isaac, and the old man and the old woman were Abraham and Sarah. He was very preoccupied with this.

I then read out the session of August 16th, 1979 [page 24].

Meltzer: You certainly had a very therapeutic impact in the first session, which he announces to you immediately, that the werewolf has been captured and the gold recovered and so on. He really settles down to some sort of communication with you in which you are working almost purely with your intuition, because the content of what he says isn't really intelligible. But the mood and the flavours are what you pick up and what you talk to him about, and he seems very gratified by this – that you are not bound to language, to the verbal level. You are willing to take language in its wider, communicative aspects and so get at his feelings about things. This is very promising really.

I read out Meltzer's comments from that time on that session, and he commented further:

Meltzer: Beginning with the ram, which is part of the Abraham and Isaac story, the end of human sacrifice, so comes the end of the werewolf, the end of his putting aside his expectation of being eaten, and preparing himself to have a different kind of experience from being devoured.

I then read out some questions sent to Dr Meltzer from that same period, together with his comments from 1979. Meltzer continued:

Meltzer: It's all impression. It's all emotional impression. I don't know if you can think of it as accurate, but it is probably close enough to make contact with, and to reassure him of your interest and your attention, which is what he needs, your interest and attention and your talking, your giving names to things and acknowledging that he is doing something important and useful.

I followed this by reading out the synthesis I sent to Dr Meltzer in 1982 [page 81].

Meltzer: I really have the impression that he is reversing the situation and putting on a performance which represents the adult world showing off to the children – their cleverness, their knowledge, their skills and their sexuality, and so on. This is a situation in which the adolescent takes revenge by doing exactly the same, particularly flaunting their sexuality, claiming to be more knowledgeable than the adult world, thrusting themselves forward politically, claiming that they would know what to do if they took over the government and so on, the terrorists, the barricades of the revolution, as it were.

I think the question is really the antics of the combined objects, showing off to the children how clever and how potent they are. It is a typical situation you see in children dressing up as adults, who they see as these actors and actresses putting on performances all the time.

I then read out a session from 1983, from the year before the analysis was scheduled to end, and point out that Mário saw the previous patient. Meltzer asked "Adult or child?" and I replied, "Child". The session went as follows:

> Mário comes in and greets me with a handshake, looking me straight in the eye. He says: "The council wishes you a pleasant journey." His eyes are filled with tears. I ask, "What's the matter, Mário? You are sad. You set out on your journey and now you are filled with sad feelings?"
>
> He doesn't answer and continues talking about the route, like a road map from São Paulo to Montevideo, until the last minutes of the session. The route contains the following map data:
>
> Miracatu, 2 kilometres
> Registro, 2 kilometres
> Jacapiranga, 22 kilometres
> We are at the city limit.

Meltzer: Does this road map have any relation to reality, the names of the towns and so on?
Mélega: No.
Meltzer: They are completely confabulated.
Mélega: Yes, but he sticks to a rhythm in the distances: 2, 2, 22, 1, as well as with the names: three names, two names, three names.
Junqueira: This makes for a kind of rhythm like that of a musical chant.
Meltzer: An incantation? Is that your interpretation?

Mélega: You are here physically, visually, sensorially, but your emotion is being eroded by the fear of arriving at and grabbing onto punch-bag-Marisa and running the risk of invasion.

Meltzer: That is what you said to him. What is the "punch-bag-Marisa"? What does this mean? Why do you refer to yourself this way?

Mélega: Because the previous week he kicked me when I interrupted.

Meltzer: So, the impression is that some sort of separation is going on and he is rehearsing some notion of distance, of going.

Participant: Was this at the end of the analysis? How much longer did he stay with you?

Mélega: Another year after this session.

Meltzer: I think this is more object relations. It is like the small child whose mother has gone out shopping and is rehearsing to himself where she is, and where she is going. "Now, she's on this street", "Now, she's at this shop", "Now, she's going there…", "Now, she's coming home", "Here she is, here she is!" It's a way of controlling. There is a patient who comes to mind; as a child she designed a route around the stove and would trace where her mother was going with her finger.

Mélega: He was mapping the object position.

Meltzer: And in this way, controlling it.

Mélega: So, basically, he hasn't changed.

Meltzer: But he is more in the object relation. He is not undertaking much reversal, with you having to watch and he performing, and so on.

Mélega: There is another behavioural tendency during the session: to write down numbers, all through the session. Continuing with this session from 1983 (it was on March 3rd), he began writing a number sequence that counts upwards along the line, then on the next line the sequence is repeated, but starting one number down from the first, for example, if the first line contained the numbers 81 to 90, the next line would start at 80 and go to 89, the third would start at 79 and go to 88, etc. I told him that the previous Monday he had written the same sequence and it seemed to me to be a path that he created in his mind to lead him back to me.

Meltzer: Yes, this is probably correct. It is very, very common for children to draw maps of how to get to the consulting room from their home. Frances Tustin had a boy who was always drawing maps and, one day, he draw a map of his home to the consulting room; another time, he drew a picture of a lion advancing on a piece of meat, and it was exactly the same picture as the map from his home to the consulting room. It really was a marvellous representation of what was, in his mind, the way from his home to the consulting room, rapacious and wanting his flesh. Frances was surprised by this.

Mélega: There is a final section in my work that I titled *Life Prospects,* which begins: "For the past two years, Mário has been participating in group sporting activities at the Community Centre, after a suggestion I made in a conversation with his parents. I advised the parents, on several occasions, to provide him with the means to expand his areas of interest and even enrol him in an apprenticeship that would suit his character and preferences" [page 96 above].

Meltzer: It happens in children with autistic beginnings who start to emerge from the autism, becoming more and more obsessive, and then their obsession seizes upon some particular activity, which is developed and developed, their interest becoming more and more focused. But the product gets more and more perfectionist and the child is on the way to becoming an *idiot savant* – an idiot who displays an exceptional skill, but within a very limited field.

We have a boy here who has become quite famous because of his drawings. He draws architectural things and he can look at a building for five seconds and then go and draw the whole thing. Without perspective. Over the years, he has drawn pictures of London and gradually destroyed the entire city, but destroyed it in the exactly the same way it was actually destroyed, with its beautiful buildings being replaced by horrible, modern architecture, and often the perspective is as if seen from an aeroplane. They are wonderful drawings. They started up a company to sell his drawings and tour with him, displaying him like a circus attraction. He was a type of *idiot savant*, in his specialization.

I then described to Meltzer the ending of Mário's analysis, his life prospects, and the two Rorschach tests done before the start and toward the end of his analysis (as detailed above). Meltzer commented:

Meltzer: This pretty much corresponds with your clinical experience of him. This talking, the rigidity of the repetition, was certainly what Mrs Bick would call a second skin. She described this in "The Gift of the Gab" – this talking, talking, talking as a way of creating a second skin in children with an early autistic disorder, not necessarily right at the beginning, but sometime in the first three years, very often connected with the birth of the next sibling. It's a kind of reduction of one's mentality to very simple, sensual, what I call dismantled level, where there are no objects, there are only sensations, and of course, the repetitiveness has the function of perception in ordinary development. Instead of the perception of objects, they produce these repetitive phenomena which function as if they were objects, and by these means, they remain relatively free of anxiety by producing ritualised behaviour, instead of anxiety, instead of emotions.

Mélega: It's another kind of world.

Meltzer: It is not even really a world. It is just a blur of unintegrated sensations in which the different senses are not related to one another, and nothing becomes three-dimensional. It tends to remain very two-dimensional, and object relations, at best, are very adhesive, superficial, and they cling with their eyes, their ears, their noses.

[*An unrecorded remark.*]

Meltzer: Yes. It is, in a certain sense, an adventure in another modality of life. And sometimes, as I said in the case of the "idiot savant", they really do develop and produce something of value, or we invest it with value. The boy who drew buildings – his drawings have no artistic value, but they are so exact, so accurate, precise and so photographic that we wondered how he does it. Could he have some kind of internal photographic process?

Mélega: In this case, perhaps one of his senses was highly developed?

Meltzer: Exactly. His sense of sight was developed like a camera. He took photographs in his mind and reproduced them wonderfully and quickly.

Mélega: It's easier when you don't have to combine all the senses to "perceive" the object. Because in an autistic state, the senses are separate from each other.

Meltzer: Yes, because the autistic doesn't see things with meaning. He sees them concretely and factually, and this boy who makes these architectural drawings is completely unimaginative. When he does add imaginary elements, which are almost always that a building has caught fire, they really take on certain autistic qualities: the flames are shooting out of the windows, people are jumping out of them, and so on. But, the result is that this building is eradicated and is then replaced by an ugly piece of plastic. All of London was replaced in this way. His destructiveness has more vitality than anything else. The flames shooting out of the windows look very realistic and have a lot of movement.

Mélega: Is it correct to assume that you are distinguishing three different worlds: the autistic world, the projective identification worlds, and the world of the symbolic mind?

Meltzer: Certainly. I use the concept of "world" very much in relation to the world of projective identification, the world of the delusional system and the world of imaginative perception. Whether it's right to think of the autistic as having a world, I'm not sure, because it is so unintegrated and so devoid of meaning that I am not really sure that I would call it a world. Nothing develops, nothing really happens, and very often, one sees that there is an element of *folie-à-deux* between the child and the parents, when they are involved. For instance, one young boy who had autism and became extremely obsessive, fixated completely on the idea that he wanted to see his therapist's breasts and begged her to take off her clothes. When, after a few months, it became clear that she wasn't going to do this, he decided to create another therapist, which he proceeded to do with bits of clothes junk collected from near his home and with his father's help. He began to construct a delusional object. It began to invade the playroom, which had been appointed with various functions, like listening and remembering. Finally, he got disappointed that his alternative therapist was not as beautiful as his actual one, who was, in fact, a lovely girl from Finland. So, he decided that if she wouldn't take off her clothes to show him her breasts, and if he couldn't build an object as beautiful as she was, he would instead build a telescope with which he could see the dome of Saint Paul's Cathedral. The trouble with this was that he didn't have a line of sight from his home, because his window wasn't high enough, so he had to build a periscope and his father helped him in the task. He was very, very pleased with this because the periscope was finished at around the same time that his therapist had to go back to Finland.

Mélega: Do you see and understand the boy's movement as his getting to grips with a problem of symbol formation, or just as one of projective identification with the breast-object in its sensory dimension?

Meltzer: Neither. There is an absolute lack of symbol formation: the absolute concreteness of the thing in itself, the object and its sensory impact, not its erotic impact, not its aesthetic impact, or its spiritual impact. For instance, for the Japanese, Mount Fuji has a spiritual impact. For the autistic child, it is purely a sensory impact, an image.

Mélega: But, when he changes his interest from seeing the therapist's breasts to looking at the dome, could this movement be understood as the beginning of symbol formation?

Meltzer: It is not symbol formation. It is a substitute. It is breast-shaped, that's all.

Mélega: It's an equation?

Meltzer: It's a symbolic equation.

Reflections from January, 1998

During the first two years of analysis with Mário, I was unable to have the normal interaction and contact with his unconscious that I was used to having with other patients. This lack of contact and his acting as a reporter-actor-commentator who talked to an audience – his defences against contact – rendered his analysis very difficult and what I wanted was to knock down these defences so that the baby-who-became-an-autistic child could appear. In my opinion, the defensive organization that he set in place when he moved out of autism was one of rigidity, repetition and unshakeable inaccessibility.

The baby's short-lived vital manifestations (the part of Mário's personality that was in touch with other human beings) raised doubts about baby-Mário being alive and left me to face the gorilla, demystifying it and fighting against its false grandiosity, which was, in fact, blocking the "rescue" of the baby – the portion of Mário's psychic life that was alive. So I can understand my gathering forces and attack on the Mário-gorilla: I often tried to be the super-hero-baby who will overcome the gorilla. And it is from this position that I can understand all the "explorations" and "acting" that I took as coming from the non-acceptance of what proved itself to be the depth and extensiveness of Mário's personality split. Furthermore, the behaviour I noticed in the room (which I managed to describe to Dr Meltzer sufficiently well for him to be able to provide meanings) had for me no meaning in its content, and I saw it purely as a defence against contact and emotional experience. In fact, I often felt him to be so distant that I doubted whether there was, in fact, any transference developing. There can be no doubt that the meanings Dr Meltzer provided me with regarding the material I sent him made me gradually more capable of theorizing on the basis of the clinical material, with Klein as a reference, already at that time (1978) enriched by Bion's contributions about maternal *reverie* and the mother–baby relationship.

However, I had a technical resistance that persisted for a long time in this analysis and that consisted of assuming an interventionist stance, a posture contrary to the analytical one that I had adopted until then. I do recognize that many times I made interventions that seemed to be *acting-in* due to my anxiety to "save the baby". Many times, intolerance to this anxiety, in addition to impotence about the fact that my interpretations did not change the state of Mário-gorilla's mind, led me to give up analysing him; under these extreme circumstances Mário provided me with a response that showed his desire and need to continue.

Dr Meltzer pointed out the need to fight for room in order to "exist analytically". This happened during the sessions when I thought aloud, acted-out, threatened to leave the room, or suggested we end the analysis.

I would like to propose some considerations on technique for cases of this severity, where there are serious limitations for the development of a symbolic mind – an incapacity to learn due to the impossibility of being, and continuing to be, in the emotional experience, so that changes can occur in meanings and symbols. This impossibility results from the patient's imposition of cutting off any contact that becomes intolerable, as a result of the lack of any internal space where several elements of the experience can be accommodated and united to create meanings.

In other words, what Mário is "able to think" during a relationship situation is so adverse, so crude and rigid, with neither alternatives nor escape routes, that he can only isolate himself in his world of stories. It seems then, that it is necessary to surround the therapeutic situation *from all sides*: giving meaning to the contents of his communications, showing him his thought models, taking care of a baby – his living portion – and fighting against the gorilla part's arrogance and grandiosity.

Lastly, perhaps we should consider what I called my countertransference not simply as my own emotional situation: the intolerance of impotence when faced with his defence of "gorilla stupidity". As it was impossible to analyse this part, I tried to systematically focus my attention on the "moribund baby", his incipient symbolic mind that was in danger of becoming stagnant.

However, we must not lose sight of the fact that such a patient, who systematically fails to establish a relationship, provokes feelings that must be differentiated from feelings of personal countertransference and be understood as reactions to a patient who fails to take part in the analysis, who is uncooperative or unable to cooperate. We must consider it as a situation when the patient is not using the analyst as a container for his projective identifications, and so the analyst cannot perform his role of an external container object.

REFERENCES

Bick, E. (1968). The experience of the skin in early object relations. *International Journal of Psychoanalysis*, 49: 484-86. Reprinted in: M. H. Williams (Ed.), *The Tavistock Model: Papers on Child Development and Psychoanalytic Training by Martha Harris and Esther Bick,* pp. 133-38. London: Harris Meltzer Trust, 2011.

Bion, W. R. (1962). A Theory of Thinking. In: *Second Thoughts*, pp. 110-119. London: Maresfield Library.

Bion, W. R. (1970). *Attention and Interpretation.* London: Tavistock.

Heimann, P. (1950). On countertransference. *International Journal of Psycho-Analysis* 31: 81-84.

Klein, M. (1975 [1946]). Notes on Some Schizoid Mechanisms. In: *Envy and Gratitude and Other Works 1946-1963*, pp. 1-24. London: Hogarth Press.

Klein, M. (1975 [1961]). *Narrative of a Child Analysis: The Conduct of the Psychoanalysis of Children as seen in the Treatment of a Ten-year-old Boy* London: Hogarth Press. Reprinted London: Karnac, 1992.

Meltzer, D. (1968). An interruption technique for the analytic impasse. In: *Sincerity: Collected Papers of Donald Meltzer*, ed. A. Hahn, pp. 152-165. London: Karnac, 1994.

Meltzer, D. (1975). *Explorations in Autism: A Psychoanalytical Study.* Perthshire: Clunie Press for the Roland Harris Educational Trust. Reprinted London: Harris Meltzer Trust, 2008.

Meltzer, D. (1986). *Studies in Extended Metapsychology: Clinical Applications of Bion's Ideas.* Reprinted London: Harris Meltzer Trust, 2008.

Tustin, F. (1972). *Autism and Childhood Psychosis.* London: Hogarth Press.

Tustin, F. (1980). Autistic objects. In: *International Review of Psycho-Analysis* 7: 27-39.

adhesive identification 19, 22, 23, 66, 67, 70, 109

adolescent community 83

analytical relationship
    container 97, 113
    exploration *vs* control 84
    feeding 25, 45, 50, 53, 55-56, 64, 70, 82, 96
    "here and now" 11
    "rubbish bin"/ toilet 64, 87
    "talking" analyst 44
    technical problems 21, 43ff, 82, 111
    see also object, internal/ analytical

autism, infantile ix, xi, 1-3, 22, 69, 70, 81, 111

autistic object 18, 66, 71ff

baby, in analysis 7, 14, 28, 30, 35, 44, 54, 57, 58, 73, 80, 83, 84, 90, 93, 95-96, 112
    greed of 59

out of contact 19, 33
paranoid 56
and penis 29
    see also transference

Bick, Esther xi, 22, 67
    second skin 76, 97, 108

Bion, Wilfred 29, 47, 59, 62, 84
    basic assumption 87
    beta-screen 31, 34
    common sense 22
    learning from experience 59
    maternal reverie 75, 111
    "super"-ego 55

body-ego 62, 68

claustrophobia 50, 91

countertransference xi, 7, 63, 84, 84, 112
    see also transference

defences 7-9, 14, 24, 31, 40, 44, 60, 61, 63, 68, 95, 98, 99, 111
    autistic x, 67, 72

disturbed 29
  obsessive 17, 19, 69, 96
  of "gorilla" stupidity 112
  through reversal 59
depressive anxiety 22, 37, 50, 81,
    93
  escape from 37
  persecutory 24
depressive position 95, 59, 60, 64
dismantling (Meltzer) xi, 21, 22,
    108
dreams, stories as 60
Freudian slip 7
hallucination 31, 60
Harris, Martha x, 18ff
idealization, mother–baby 26, 27,
    28, 30, 36, 44, 68, 70
Kierkegaard, Soren 33
Klein, Melanie x, 21, 59, 66, 111
  and Bion 84
  "breast that feeds itself" 55
learning
  disorder 1
  practical 77
  see also school
Maberino de Prego, Vida 19
Mário's development
  early 1-3, 74ff
  "gorilla" xi, 31-36, 39, 51, 55-
    56, 112-113
  obsessionality xi, 67, 87
  puppet-like 2, 5, 12, 19, 32,
    36, 61, 62, 65, 68
masturbation 66, 81
Meltzer, Donald, books
  Explorations in Autism ix, xi,
    19, 21, 66,
  The Psychoanalytical Process 59
mindlessness xi, 22
  and group dynamics 87
Money-Kyrle, Roger 62, 68
mother's depression/ failure x, 22,

    75
mutism 14, 22, 103
narcissistic identification 22
  and body functions 23
  organization 60
object, internal/ analytical 5, 15,
    19, 38, 68, 70, 92, 97, 110,
    113
  combined/ whole 53, 57, 105
  controlled 87, 108
  delusional 110
  destroyed/ damaged 17, 30,
    100
  idealized 59, 66, 67
  imprisoned 69
  maternal x, 22
  speaking 23, 85
  transitional 61, 62
    see also analytic relation-
      ship; autistic object; part-
      object
obsessionality xi, 67, 87
Oedipal feelings 23, 27, 28, 29,
    30, 91
omnipotent control 5, 6, 22, 27,
    29, 44, 47, 53, 55, 64, 68, 79,
    92, 93
  and basic assumption 87
  by mapping the object 107
  by naming 49
  and projective identification
    76
  reversal of 95
  and symbolic equation 69
  and tyranny 7, 79, 87, 100
    see also Mario's develop-
      ment; obsessionality
paranoia 29, 51, 52, 56
part-object 24, 25, 27, 29, 55, 68
persecutory feelings 24, 50, 51, 56,
    59, 60, 66, 96, 100
post-autism 19, 22, 70, 87, 89, 97

preverbal language 20, 84
projection and introjection 19,
    22, 23, 45, 63, 64, 67, 70,
    76, 97
    and mental pain 84
Rorschach test 98ff
school 15, 49ff, 77
    camp 40
    of mother's inside 50
    schoolmates 39
    special (CIAM) 3, 43, 65
separation, difficulty 22, 29,
    45, 59, 61, 64, 68, 69, 93,
    106
space, internal 22, 66, 70, 97, 112
    for contact xi, 9, 29, 63, 68,
    72, 79, 82
splitting-and-idealization 59, 66,
    67
 symbol formation xi, 59, 63, 97,

109, 112
    vs signs 47
    vs symbolic equation 69, 75,
    109
telenovela 60
transference x, 7, 19-20, 22, 27,
    32, 34, 59, 68, 69, 87, 111
    acting in 39, 61
    vs transitional object 62
        see also countertransference
Tustin, Frances 72, 81, 107
two-dimensional object 66, 87,
    108
    vs tri-dimensional 19
verbalization xi, 7, 18, 30, 68-69,
    85
    and vocalization 23
        see also preverbal language
weaning 33, 34, 95, 96
Winnicott, Donald 87